DEFILED

The Spiritual Dangers of Alternative Medicine

KEN MCDONALD B.D., Th.M.

Ken McDonald Evangelistic Ministries
You may contact us at:
www.kenmcdonaldfamily.com

ISBN: 1453748695
ISBN-13: 9781453748695

CONTENTS

PREFACE

What? know ye not that your body is the temple of the Holy Ghost which is in you, which ye have of God, and ye are not your own?

1Cor. 6:19

Wherefore, as I live, saith the Lord GOD; Surely, because thou hast defiled my sanctuary with all thy detestable things, and with all thine abominations, therefore will I also diminish thee; neither shall mine eye spare, neither will I have any pity.

Ezek. 5:11

ACKNOWLEDGEMENTS

I want to especially thank Alice, along with Lori who took the time to warn Terri and I of the error of our way. I would also like to thank Pastor Ray, and Pastor Jeff whom God used in a great way one Sunday evening to confirm to me by the word of God to continue to expose the wickedness of Alternative Medicine. I would also like to thank Dennis whom God used expressly one Sunday morning to confirm to me to write this book. I would also like to thank Ed, Paul, Andrew, Paul Debbie and Jim, Mark "the perfect man", Fred, Brad, Marshall, Jim, Jesse, Bill, as well as many others who have been a great help and encouragement in the writing of this book.

I would also like to thank my wife Terri for her love for her Saviour, the Lord Jesus Christ, and her desire to have a right heart and relationship with Him. Without that we may never have gotten out of the snare that we were caught in.

Blessed be the LORD, who hath not given us as a prey to their teeth.
Our soul is escaped as a bird out of the snare of the fowlers: the snare is broken, and we are escaped.
Our help is in the name of the LORD, who made heaven and earth.
Psalm 124:6-8

INTRODUCTION

The mountain air was crisp and cold. The smell of smoke wafted through the hills from the fireplaces as they burned the wood to heat the homes. That certain excitement filled the air for it was Christmas, and family had come to the small simple house of the young couple. Their two children grinned with excitement to see all of the presents, though the youngest, a girl, was only a year and a half old.

They had a fine traditional meal with turkey, stuffing, and all of the trimmings. One by one the presents were opened and the family mused over the gifts. To the "grown-ups" the greatest present was to behold the joy on the faces of the children as they opened their presents. It was a time of joy, love, and contentment.

By now the presents had been opened and supper had been enjoyed. The family, with loved ones there, sat around the living room, talked and enjoyed the closeness, the love, and the sense of belonging that comes when family is together. With bellies full of good food Mom and Dad, Grandma and Grandpa with the others, sat contented and watched the kids play with their new toys while the family talked about old times.

Then, in the strangest sort of way, the young blond haired bright eyed girl, clothed in a footed sleeper, and with a pacifier in her mouth ran across the living room, stopped, and with the brightest happiest eyes started gibbering through her pacifier. She then ran to the other side of the living room, in front of everyone and squealed with some more Jibber Jabber. Back she ran again, and by this time everyone was watching her, trying to figure out what she was doing. Once again she stopped and with the greatest joy in her eyes she gibbered through her pacifier again. This happened about five or six times. The family laughed as they watched, for her joy was infectious and caused great amusement, and fond memories for the family that Christmas evening. But they never knew what made her do what she did.

Years passed and one day when the young girl was now a teenager, the family was sitting and talking about memories of the past few years. To children it seems so long and yet for mom and dad it's just a few years. As they talked and laughed about the memories, her dad began to tell about that Christmas evening when his baby girl ran back and forth with such joy. He told of how everyone laughed as they watched her run back and forth.

To his surprise the girl, now a young teenager spoke up and said that she remembered that evening. Mom, Dad and brother mentioned other particulars of the night to make sure it was the same one that the young girl was now talking about and it was. She told them that she remembered that a thought struck her and filled her with joy. She told how the thought came into her mind that she was alive, and life had just begun. She would run across the room, stop and what she was joyful about was the realization that she was alive, and life had just begun. She then would run back to the other side of the living room and joyfully squeal and laugh and in gibberish, that at the time could not be understood, yet she was proclaiming with great joy that she was alive, and life had just begun.

There are three natural drives in man. The strongest drive in you is the desire to stay alive, to reproduce is second and the third is to enjoy yourself. In the word of God, Satan and the Lord are discussing the man named Job. In that conversation Satan declares, *"Skin for skin, yea, all that a man hath will he give for his life."* (Job 2:4) Though spoken by Satan, yet it is a general truth. Down through the ages there have been examples of people who have given the ultimate sacrifice for others, yet they are the exception.

I remember hearing of the concentration camps in Germany during World War II. Jews were brought there to be exterminated. Like cattle they were directed to go into a building not knowing they would never come out alive. In that building they were gassed and killed. After the gassing they would have to remove the bodies. As they opened the doors, there on the floor were piles of dead bodies. Crushed on the bottom of the pile were the children. Above them were the women, and above them, on top of the dead pile of bodies were the men. In their last gasps for air, the strongest climbed to the top in order to have one more breath of life.

Life, the desire to live and stay alive, the desire to take another breath, open your eyes once again, and to live another day. That desire, that drive spurns us onward day after day, yet time and the motions of sin wear us down with each passing moment. We travel through time seeking to live long and to live well, yet at the end of our journey lies an open grave waiting for our body to be placed into it, and as they say, we will be put to bed with a shovel. Some day we will breathe our last breath, our heart will beat its last beat, and we shall leave these vessels of clay. Some shall leave for Heaven, and some shall leave for Hell.

I think of the martyrs who were killed because they would not confess what their tormentors wanted them to confess. As well as other stories where a love for their God or fellow man transcended their desire to stay alive and they willingly gave their life that another might continue to live and live well.

> *Lord Schilik was about fifty years of age, and was possessed of great natural and acquired abilities. When he was told he was to be quartered, and his parts scattered in different places, he smiled with great serenity, saying, "The loss of a sepulcher is but a trifling consideration." A gentleman who stood by was crying, "Courage, my lord!" he replied, "I have God's favor which is sufficient to inspire any one with courage: the fear of death does not trouble me; formerly I have faced him in fields of battle to oppose Antichrist; and now dare face him*

> *on a scaffold, for the sake of Christ." Having said a short prayer, he told the executioner he was ready. He cut off his right hand and his head, and then quartered him. His hand and his head were placed upon the high tower of Prague and his quarters distributed in different parts of the city.* (John Fox, Foxe's Book of Martyrs, Accordance Bible Program - Public Domain, Chapter VIII: An Account of the Persecutions in Bohemia Under the Papacy).

While Lord Schilik gave his life because of his Saviour, and others have given their lives, yet those who continue day to day have a drive to live and to live well.

To not merely live, but to live well, embraces the ever-consuming desire to live like a young man and his bride, like a mother and her newborn, or like ivy on a wall. There is the longing to live well and be free from pain, shortness of breath, and any other condition that would steal our comfort like a thief in the night. Sickness is like that thief at times. It steals our health so that now this life, while still clung to, is no longer the joy to live that it once was. It is now a challenge, a labor, and a valley that seems so deep we wonder why we would even want to continue. Yet that desire to live drives us on in hope of climbing out the other side to once again take a breath without pain, or to spend a night in restful sleep.

With such a desire, those who claim to have the answers for you to keep good health thus enabling you to enjoy your life, or those who claim to have the answers so that you will be able to prolong your life, are highly esteemed. They are often sought out with great diligence in your quest to live this life, and to live it well. Word of mouth travels quickly as new remedies are found. People tell others out of a desire to help them out of the pain sorrow and hurt that even they themselves once new. Yes, solutions travel fast, often by word of mouth.

It did not take long for the multitudes to learn of the healing powers of the Lord Jesus Christ. They sought him out.

> *And when they were gone over, they came into the land of Gennesaret. And when the men of that place had knowledge of him, they sent out into all that country round about, and brought unto him all that were diseased; And besought him that they might only touch the hem of his garment: and as many as touched were made perfectly whole.* Matthew14:34-36

Down through the centuries, many different remedies have been tried. Some of them were merely opportunists seeking to make some money. Other remedies were sincere experiments in hope of truly helping someone, yet the medicine was faulty thus providing no help, and may even have harmed the patient. All for the purpose to fulfill the ever consuming desire to live, and to live well.

Over the past six thousand years this desire to live and to live well has motivated man to seek cures for sickness. Peering through that darkness, just out of view, slithering in the shadows is a subtle old creature. With eyes of fury he peers out of the darkness at his subjects whom he knows better than they know themselves. He knows their ever-strong desire to live, and to live well. With a thirst for blood and a hatred for God, he plots, as Jesus Christ said, to kill, to steal, and to destroy those for whom the Good Shepherd died. The king of terrors seeks men, women, boys and girls, and many times he will enter by the open door at the desire to live, and to live well.

Camouflaged with good works, and deceived through the blindness that comes from a lack of knowledge of the word of God, the old deceiver sends his workers out to "help" the sick when in reality they are propagating witchcraft and bringing about the destruction of those people, saved or lost, who blindly stumble into, and become ensnared in this medicine that blocks the blessing of God on a saint as when Delilah cut Samson's hair.

In the following pages I will seek, by the grace of God, to show the satanic influence, and the unbiblical application of alternative medicine. There is no doubt in my mind that his medicine is warned against in the scriptures. A Christian who uses or practices this medicine will loose the blessing of the Lord Jesus Christ on their life, their family, as well as their church. Jesus Christ said, *"Without me, ye can do nothing."* (John 15:5)

When the Lord Jesus Christ steps back from you the result is destruction.

Man is naturally self-destructive and needs an external power to reach within him and pull him up. It's like water, which runs downhill. You need a power greater than yourself to pick you up. This comes in different forms. Regeneration is one of the ways in which this is accomplished by being born again through the Lord Jesus Christ. The second way is by revival, where the Lord Jesus Christ picks you up and revives you spiritually so as to enable you to serve Him, walk with Him, and be pleasing in His sight. It is a spiritual renewal.

To lose God's help and blessing in and on your life is to fail in your walk with Him. His desire is to fellowship with you because spiritually, if you are saved, you are already married to Him. The Bible says, *"He that is joined unto the Lord is one spirit."* (1 Cor. 6:17), and the Lord loves you. But to entertain unclean spirits in the attempt to heal your spiritually crucified body is to commit spiritual fornication, and it grieves your Saviour greatly. You are cheating on your Saviour!

He steps back and will not fellowship with you until you confess your sins and repent. But if you confess them, He is faithful and just to forgive you of your sins and to cleanse you from all unrighteousness. Praise the Lord He is faithful!

My wife Terri, and I, stumbled and fell into this witchcraft that I am about to write about. With broken hearts we confessed our sins, repented and faithful as always, our great Saviour, Jesus

Christ forgave us, picked us up and revived our walk with Him.

What follows is of utmost importance! Witchcraft in the form of medicine is sweeping through the churches and spiritually killing them.

One day a botanist took a break from his work studying the plants and animals and sat down under the shade of a great tree. He took out his lunch and began to enjoy a sandwich. The sun was shining, birds were heard singing, and his senses filled with the sights and sounds of the nature that he loved to study. Not long after sitting down he noticed a few feet away a sundew plant. It is a plant that has special leaves that have prongs on them with droplets of sweet dew sitting on top of each prong. The Dew is sweet and sticky, and it is a trap. Because of the lack of minerals in the soil the Lord designed these plants to eat flies. The flies get caught as they lick the dew of the leaf.

The botanist noticed a fly that had just landed on the leaf, and began to lick the sweet dew. As the fly moved a leg more prongs stuck to it. Then a wing, and another leg got stuck to the sweet prongs. With each prong attaching to the fly, the leaf began to slowly fold itself around the fly. The fly struggled little, but more and more it was entangled and devoured by the plant. As the last little bit of the fly could be seen, the botanist noticed, it was still licking the dew. What seemed so sweet and good was really its destruction.

Chapter

1

MY INTRODUCTION INTO NEW AGE MEDICINE

Over the past thirty years my wife Terri and I have had many remedies suggested to us, and many, which we have tried. In our younger years we were much more gullible and easily persuadable to try these various remedies.

One of the first was while we were still in Bible School and I had an ear infection. It seemed there was always some sort of new remedy going around or someone who had information on natural remedies. We found out that the remedy for an ear infection was to put onions in the ear. The theory was that they would draw the infection out of the ear and into the onions.

Well, my wife chopped up the onions, not too small, and put them in my ear. A piece of cotton gauze and tape was then affixed over my ear. It bulged out a bit because my ear was full of onions. It did not work as my infection got worse and I remember having the taste of onions in my mouth the whole time. I know onions are not good for your breath but they made my ear smell too. I could eat a hamburger with no onions on it though; the problem was if I had oatmeal. It just did not go together well.

Another "remedy" was the time I tried wild peach leaves in order to cure my allergy to Poison Oak. Oh My!

There in the beautiful mountains of California grows a bush called poison oak. Above 4,000' elevation it does not grow. We lived at 3,500' elevation so it grew very well. Upon moving into our house in 1993, I noticed that our yard was full of poison oak bushes, well, not full, but there were many of them

The house was built on the side of a hill with the front side of the house at ground level and the backside of the house one and a half stories above the ground. This was not unusual for a house in the mountains. On the side of that hill were many bushes of poison oak.

My first thought was that I needed to eradicate my property of the poison oak. If our dog walked through them, or if one of our kids touched them then they would get poison oak as well, and I did not want this to happen. So I decided that I would be extra careful and put long sleeves on held at the wrists with rubber bands. A hat, boots, and that I would only touch the poison oak by pruning it with shears and picking it up also with those shears and putting it all in a pile.

With utmost care and caution I proceeded to clear the poison oak away. When done I immediately took a cold shower and washed with strong soap. With all of this care taken I still got covered with red itchy pocks of poison oak. This astonished me to no end after the care I had taken. Well, I was miserable so I went to the store to find something to treat it with.

While there I ran into an old timer of the area that I knew by the name of Mr. Waltz. Not having seen him for many years I said hello and we talked for a short time. I then mentioned that I was there to pick up something for my poison oak and he then replied, "You ought to get some wild peach leaves." Well, I had never heard of wild peach leaves so he showed me these rather tough bushy weeds that were growing on the side of the hill that surrounded the parking lot we were standing in. He said, "The Indians used this to cure them of their allergy to poison oak. If you will suck on these leaves for two weeks you will not be allergic to poison oak any more."

This excited me for I have been allergic to poison oak all my life. I thanked him and then proceeded to go cut and collect a nice juicy bunch of fresh wild peach leaves. They were a dark forest green in color, and about six inches long but only a half and inch wide, with scalloped edges. They were shiny on top and a dull light grey green on the bottom.

Upon arriving home, and with eager anticipation that I was going to be cured of my allergy, I rinsed the leaves thoroughly in water. Then with my wife, son and daughter watching I rolled a leaf up, placed it into my mouth and chomped down on it so as to crush it so the juice would flow out. Well, that juice was the bitterest thing I have ever eaten in my life. I wanted to spit it out right there on the spot, but my desire to be cured of poison oak was great so I sucked on that leaf and swallowed the bitter juice. My teeth turned green with pieces of sticky leaf stuck to them. I cleaned the chewed up leaf remnant out and put another one in and sucked on it.

After a couple of days of trying to ingest wild peach leaf juice I decided to go to the doctor where upon he prescribed some shots for me. They were shots of pure poison oak extract and they really worked. I have not been nearly as allergic to poison oak since those shots. Maybe if I had endured two weeks of sucking on bitter wild peach leaves I would have overcome my allergy to poison oak? But I don't think so.

Some years after that the Lord led me into the field of evangelism, and I have traveled, and still do, week after week preaching in various churches. The Lord has greatly blessed this and it wasn't long before I was preaching fifty-two weeks a year, about seven times a week. That adds up to a lot of preaching. What happened though was that my voice was not able to hold up under the demand that I was putting it through. Little by little it was getting worse. Again, remedies were suggested for me to try to help my voice. Room temperature water during preaching, or room temperature unsweetened tea with lemon, Sen-Sen (an old licorice breath candy), slippery elm lozenges, Fisherman's Friend cough drops. The all time worst "remedy" for my throat was the fresh juice of one lemon in a glass with as much cayenne pepper as one can stand. It was like a shot of I don't know what! That one had me choking, gagging, and screaming all at the same time.

As my voice was growing weaker and weaker other people would suggest things. While at one church the pastor's wife suggested that I go to the naturopathic doctor that she had gone to. She highly recommended him, so I went to him. While there he looked at my whole family. I had never been to a doctor like this before, but others I knew had gone to him and highly recommended him as well. These were good faithful Christians so my confidence in them eased any concerns I had about going to a naturopathic doctor.

Since he was an iridologist the first thing he did was to start scrying the iris of my eye. (I will explain this later.) This took a while as he peered on the iris of my eye and then wrote various circles and signs that suggested to him various diagnoses of my body. You know, the strange thing about it was that he did not have anything to say about my voice. Zip, zero, nada! And I told him that it was bad. I was not hiding anything from him yet he had no help for my voice whatsoever.

After the scrying of my iris, he then began to muscle test me for various substances. This was to diagnose allergies and incompatibilities to various substances. I do not remember all the things he tested me for except one and that was chocolate.

His office consisted of the front corner of a small health food store. There were two windows in the front of the store with the entrance door between them. As you entered the store there was a small table and chair to the right and this is where he treated his patients. For the muscle testing I was standing with my right hand held straight out palm up. My left arm was held out as well with the palm down. He placed the vials of substances in my right hand. Then he would lightly push down on my left hand. If I could resist his light downward pressure then I was not allergic to the substance, but if I could not resist then I was allergic to the substance, according to him.

The strangest sensation happened when he placed the small glass vial of chocolate in my right hand. I felt a magnetic like sensation jolt the palm of my right hand. I say magnetic but it almost felt like a slight gust of wind inside my hand that started as a large circle around my hand and then closed into the center of my hand where the small vial of chocolate was held. It was so strange a sensation to me that when he was done I asked him to do it again so as to determine what it was. It was a curious sensation to me as he practiced the art of muscle testing that day.

He then tested my whole family and prescribed a bunch of supplements. Supplements for which we did not have the money but we bought them anyway. One of the worst he prescribed was a kind of special dirt for my wife to take. That's right, Dirt! You may ask, "Did the supplements help?" And the answer is no! Did the dirt help? NO! I'm sure for some people they have helped and do help, but for us they did not help at all.

About eight years passed by from when we went to the Naturopathic doctor and were muscle tested. Our allergies continued to trouble us at times and in the various churches remedies were recommended to us. The trouble we endured from the allergies was not all that bad for we had learned what we could eat and not eat. My voice was restored through special exercises I learned to do and though it was a great trial for a while, yet it is doing well now.

Every now and then my wife would get into some milk, usually at a restaurant where they did not listen very well as to what she could eat. One such episode caused us to take Terri to the emergency room for help because the allergy was so bad it ended with conjunctivitis.

This caused us to be more open to finding help for her allergies. I was holding meetings for a church and all was going very well. We were having a good time and while out to dinner it was recommended to us that Terri, my wife, ought to try a certain Chiropractor for her allergies. Allergies seemed to be an unrelated malady in the realm of Chiropractic medicine, but we were told of a man who had severe allergies and after being treated by this certain doctor that the allergies were gone.

I asked how this happened and was told that the doctor has a way to reset your system electrically. It's kind of like rebooting your computer. This sounded really weird to us but the person told us that it worked for them and that Terri ought to give it a try.

That night we prayed about it and decided that if the money came in to go then Terri would go and be treated for her allergies. Though the money did not come in at the allotted time, which should have given us a clue, yet, when she called to cancel the appointment it was told her that the office visit was already covered so come on in.

A couple of days later Terri went to this Chiropractor to get treated for her allergies. The Doctor is a born again Christian, and we had many good Christians recommend this treatment, or treatments like it in many of the churches that we are in. With such a common recommendation I stayed home and did not go with my wife to the treatment, but I will relate it as she has told me.

When she walked into the treatment room the doctor, a very nice lady, asked her to lie down on the patient table. Then the doctor had her hold up her left arm so it was pointing straight up. (The method is irrelevant, for it is all muscle testing, but I am relating it anyway for the information this story will reveal is relevant to the subject of this book.) As with the other Naturopathic doctor, small glass vials of substances were brought out for testing. The doctor then would place a vial of a various substance on her stomach. She then would lightly press forward down on her left arm. Some vials she could resist, and when it came to milk she could not resist and her arm went right down. To the doctor this meant that Terri was allergic to milk. Well, Terri already knew that.

Once this was determined then there was a jar like a small goldfish bowl and a bunch of the little vials were placed inside this bowl. Terri was then told to hold it in her right hand and the doctor took a small instrument that looked like a laser pointer, but the light it shined was a very bright white light. With the goldfish bowl of vials in Terri's right hand the doctor then shined this bright white light into Terri's naval (belly button) for about one minute. The doctor and she then talked for ten to fifteen minutes.

After the talk the doctor then took the goldfish bowl out of her hand and told her to rub her hands together like she was washing them with soap and water. Then she said not to eat any milk products for twenty-five hours.

Due to the sickness from milk my wife told the doctor that she was not going to eat any milk products until she could come back and be tested to see if the treatment had "held." So an appointment was made for three days later.

That night as she slept Terri had a nightmare. She dreamt that she was talking to the Devil, which in and of itself it terrified her. But what was more was that the Devil was accusing her (Rev. 12:10) of enjoying the attention she gets from the special arrangements that have to be made on her account just to eat, such as when all the dinner guests become silent as they listen to her give her special order for her food. Well, Satan is a liar (Jn 8:44) and the exact opposite is true for Terri is very uncomfortable when this happens. So in her dream she was arguing with the Devil about this for some time before he finally left.

The day before she was due to go back to the doctor to see if the treatment held she was getting ready to do her morning devotions, which is to read her daily portion out of her Bible, and then spend time in prayer. As she was getting ready for this, all of a sudden a great fear gripped her. It was a fear that she had never had before in her life. It was a fear that her allergies were going to attack her with a vengeance like never before. She got on her knees and crawled over to the couch and began to pray, *"Father I plead the blood of the Lord Jesus Christ. I know you have not given me the spirit of fear, but of power and of love and of a sound mind."* Her prayer, with tears and fervency, continued like this for about fifteen minutes when the fear finally went away.

The next day she returned to the doctor and told her of her nightmare that she had the first night after the treatment. The doctor, with a look of incredulity stated, "That's the strangest one that I have heard so far." This astonished Terri as it showed that this was a common result of the treatment. One of the workers in the office later stated that it was common for them to hear of patients telling of strange dreams and nightmares after being treated.

So now she tested Terri to see if the treatment "held." The vials of milk products were again placed into the goldfish bowl and the goldfish bowl was this time, placed in her right hand. The doctor then had Terri hold out her left hand and put her first finger and her thumb together with the palm up. It was just like the people do that practice Yoga. The first finger and the thumb make a circle. The doctor then lightly pressed down on her left hand as a muscle test and Terri could resist.

She then had her touch her second, or middle finger with her thumb. With light pressure again the doctor pushed downward on her left hand and Terri had the strength to resist. She then had Terri touch her third, or ring finger with her thumb and when the doctor pushed lightly downward, Terri could not resist and her arm went down. The doctor then stated, "You have held physically, but not emotionally." She then shined the bright light into her belly button again and told Terri that after twenty-five hours have passed she should try some milk products, but that when she did try them she was to tap, tap, tap on the middle of her forehead and as she tapped she was to repeat to herself, *"I can eat this, I can eat this."*

Red flags went off as Terri thought of how everyone in the word of God that said "I will" or "I can" did not end up well, so she then thought that she could quote the word of God and say, *"I can do all things through Christ which strengtheneth me."* (Phil. 4:13) This thought brought some peace to her mind and eased the doubt that was greatly arising in her as she recognized what seemed to be Eastern and New Age practices.

After twenty-five hours Terri tapped her forehead and said, *"I can do all things through Christ which strengtheneth me."* She then ate a cup of yogurt, and aside from some minor stomach cramps, she was all right. The next day she ate some more milk products and she was fine, each time she would tap her forehead and repeat, "I can do all things through Christ which strengtheneth me."

Let me state right here that this Eastern and New Age medicine often does work, or let me say there are results that make it appear to work. My wife, for the next four weeks, ate milk products that before the treatment would have put her in the hospital. All seemed well as she enjoyed foods that she had not dared to eat for so many years. She was able to order a regular meal and not draw attention to herself. Yet, as those first few days turned to a couple of weeks, something was different.

For me, being that I am a preacher, I noticed that my sermons did not have the power I was accustomed to discerning they had. The church services were dead, dry and discouraging. Not only this, but, I, as a preacher who loves to preach and serve the Lord Jesus Christ, had thoughts of quitting, coming off the road, and basically getting out of the ministry. This was not like me at all as I have never thought like this; or should I say I have never entertained thoughts like this for any length of time over the past thirty years. Something was different in our home and lives but it was not so drastic a change that we could put our finger on it.

The word of God states, "*For this cause shall a man leave his father and mother, and shall be joined unto his wife, and they two shall be one flesh."* (Eph. 5:31) What happens to one will have an effect on the other, and there was a general discouragement in me during this time.

Did we think it was due to her medical treatment? Not at all! The change in our home and lives was so subtle that we did not see it for the first two weeks. Looking back, Terri was the first to sense that something was wrong, and she thought it was due to some of the supplements that she was given to take after the treatment. With that thought she cut the dose in half.

But our home was different. There was an edgy, touchy, irritated spirit in our home. One that had never been there before, but it was such that you thought, "well she is just in a bad mood," or "he is down." But the depression and irritation did not go away. It lingered day after day.

One afternoon, about two weeks after the medical treatment Terri walked into the fifth-wheel trailer that is our home and as she did I said to her in a regular normal voice and tone, "You know what I think we should do? We should...'I forget what it was, but it was not some big strange thing.'" Terri looked at me and with a semi angry tone loudly stated, "No! We are not going to do that, we will do it this way!" And as she said that she backhanded me in the mid section. Immediately I with anger shouted back, "Don't you ever hit me again"!

This was not like us, as we do not treat each other this way. Terri said that when she did that she thought to herself, "*Why did I do that?*" She apologized to me and with tears in her eyes went to the bedroom and began to pray. As she prayed she said, *"Dear Lord Jesus, something is wrong. We never speak to each other this way and I don't know why I did what I did. Dear Lord please help me. Something is wrong but I don't know what it is."*

A couple more weeks went by and we traveled up to the northeast where we parked our home on wheels at a church. We had been there before, and the pastor's wife came over to see Terri. As they sat in the small living room of our RV she asked, *"So, what's new?"* Just trying to make conversation from a short lull in their talk. Terri did not want to talk about it but had nothing else to say so she said, *"Well, I am not allergic to milk products anymore."* In her reply this pastor's wife asked how did that happen? Terri told her that she had been muscle tested and that she was no longer allergic to milk products. During this conversation Terri told me later that she could sense something was going on in her body that she had never sensed before, and that there was no doubt that it was not good.

The lady then asked Terri if she would be willing to talk to someone about muscle testing? She knew of a lady that Terri needed to talk to. By now, my wife knew something was wrong and she said that she would be glad to talk to her if I gave her permission. That night she asked for permission and I said "yes," but that I would go along as well. By now even I wanted to figure out what was going on.

We were due to meet this lady at 9:00 A.M. and that morning Terri and I were fighting, yelling, slamming doors and having a real lousy time, as we got ready to go. Again Terri prayed, asking the Lord Jesus Christ for help, for she knew something was wrong. This was not the home and the marriage that we had enjoyed over the past twenty-five years. I was grouchier than a bear with a toothache, and Terri would explode quicker than an m80 in a campfire. It was not a good morning!

Well, we made it to the house where we were to meet this lady. I will call her April. April was a very nice lady, married with many children. She said that all she was going to do was give her testimony, which she did. She told of how she got into muscle testing and for the first two years her health had improved. But from then on her health declined causing her to take more and more supplements so that by the end she was taking approximately one hundred and fifty supplements a day. She was not only being muscle tested for all of this, but she was testing and treating others as well. This became her ministry.

She then told of how a little girl had appeared to her one day and then walked away, and how on another day a little boy had appeared to her and then walked away and disappeared. Strange things started happening in her home that I will not go into, but by this time her friends from church started telling her that she must get out of that medicine. April resisted this as she thought she was helping people and this was her ministry, but her life grew worse.

She said one day a Christian chiropractor made time to talk with her and he told her that she must stop muscle testing for it is divination. When she said the word divination something was shocked in my soul for I twitched slightly in astonishment at the statement. She then stated that it really is divination, but for her to quit she had this fear that she would die. Then with a big smile of peace on her face she said, "But I will just go to Heaven." And with that surrender she repented and got out of the muscle testing.

My thoughts raced for a short time. I thought to myself, "Who is this lady? What does she know?" But there was another side of me that in a still small voice said, *"You had better listen to her for she is right. It is divination."* Tears came to my eyes as I thought on the past month. Terri as well began to break as light began to break through our understanding like the sunrise after a moonless night.

We bowed our heads there at the table, and with tears in our eyes repented of our muscle testing. After thanking her for her time we went home and knelt together at our couch. I remember praying and with a broken heart confessing my sin of going to the gods of the land for help. I was aware of the spiritual dirt and shame that was on me and asked my Saviour, Jesus Christ to wash me anew in the blood of the Lamb. I felt so dirty knowing how wicked I am, and how I had grieved the Spirit of God. After some time of praying together, Terri went into the bedroom, I stayed at the couch and we prayed separately.

Later that day, about three o'clock in the afternoon I was on the couch reading my Bible when I could sense in a very real way that there was a peace, calmness, love and joy in our home that had not been there in almost a decade. Words cannot fully describe the peace that flooded our home that day, and from that day forward.

Later that night I thought to myself, what happened to us? What is this stuff they call medicine? What is going on that almost every church we are in has some of this in it in one form or another?" And so started my quest to research and find out what the word of God has to say about this New Age medicine, also known as alternative medicine, also know as Eastern Medicine. What I have found out I now put in this book. I'm sure I will learn more in the months to come, but for now there is more than enough evidence to show that what we partook of as medicine is nothing more than witchcraft.

Chapter

2

MUSCLE TESTING

There is a certain fear in man. It is the fear of the unknown. Lack of knowledge means that there are things in our lives that are out of control. Do I have cancer? Could there be cancer growing in my body right now? If it is, then it is going to kill me and I don't want to die yet, I want to live long and I want to live well. If only there was some way to satisfy my curiosity, a way to gain the knowledge if there is cancer in my body, or if there is any other disease.

If only I could find out what is going to happen to me tomorrow, or next week. Should I stay home, or should I go to work? Am I healthy right now or is there a disease growing in my body? The doctor says I'm OK, but he also said as far as we know I'm OK. But he is only a practicing physician so maybe he missed something. I don't know, I don't know, OH my, I don't know!

Knowledge of the unknown is sought for the sake of control. We desire to be in control of our lives and yet the more we seek to know the more we see what we don't know. There is a need in all of us to trust. We must put our faith and trust, based on the words of God, in the all knowing One who made us and fashioned us after his own will. We are *fearfully and wonderfully made.*

(Psa. 139:14) And the one who made us, the Lord Jesus Christ, *is able to do exceeding abundantly above all that we ask or think.* (Eph. 3:20)

Those who do not know, or do not rest in the Lord Jesus Christ are aware that their life is out of control. Whether it is their health, wealth, or especially fear of tomorrow. They trudge onward, hoping for the best, but not knowing what the morrow may bring. With examples of suffering all around, the thought for tomorrow is only allowed to be a positive one. For an example of this, just listen to your next politician who is running for office. He must make the future look bright. He must inspire hope, security, and a bright future.

Whether true or not man seeks to alleviate his fear; it is the fear of the unknown. Hence he seeks to know and to find answers to the questions he has. The problem, though, is that he wants positive answers and the word of God rarely gives the natural man positive answers. With questions such as:

Natural man: *"Where am I going when I die?"*

The word of God: *"To Hell if you are not born again."*

Natural Man: *"Well, how do I become born again?"*

The Word of God: *"You must admit that you are a sinner first of all."*

And to this the natural man recoils in rebellion and pride: *"I'm not that bad."*

He is getting knowledge, but it is not the knowledge he wants to get. It's not a knowledge that makes him feel good about himself. It's a knowledge that doesn't stroke him, so he rebels against it. That is man's nature, but this rebellion causes him to go to another source for knowledge. Another source where maybe the knowledge isn't so negative. He desires a second opinion.

You see, there are three sources of knowledge in the universe: God, Man, and Satan. All knowledge will originate from one of those three sources. God approves the first two. You have liberty to glean knowledge from God and Man, but knowledge from Satan is forbidden.

Knowledge From God

To the sincere seeking man or woman, God has made available all the knowledge they need to make it to Heaven. In the Word of God it states that Jesus Christ is *"the true Light, which lighteth every man that cometh into the world."* (Jn 1:9) According to the word of God every one is born with the knowledge of God. You don't find atheists in the Jungle, you find Atheists in the universities. You have to be "educated" out of your belief in God. *Yeah, hath God said...?* (Gen. 3:1)

Not only is every man and woman born with the knowledge of God, but the word of God again states in the book of Romans: *"For when the Gentiles, which have not the law, do by nature the things contained in the law, these, having not the law, are a law unto themselves: which shew the work of the law written in their hearts.* (Romans 2:14-15) In the book of Titus it also states: *For the grace of God that bringeth salvation hath appeared to all men.* (Titus 2:11) So man is born with much knowledge to begin with. If he acts on that knowledge then God will give him more, but if he rebels against the knowledge he has, then the light gets shut off to him, until he accepts what he already knows to be true.

You have access to all the wisdom and knowledge of the Creator of this universe right at your fingertips if you want it. With very little research there are free downloadable King James version bibles, or you can buy one at almost every Walmart, or Barnes and Nobles, and many other book stores in America, and if you don't live in America you can usually search out a missionary and get a copy of the word of God.

Yes, there are places on this earth that do not have access to a King James Bible, but chances are if you are reading this book, you are not in that condition. The King James Bible 1611 is the inerrant Word of God, and the final authority for all people alive on the earth right now. If you get yourself a copy, you will then have access to all the knowledge of God. This is true knowledge, and eternal knowledge. It is also the knowledge that all other knowledge is compared to, and where all other knowledge disagrees with what the Word of God says, then that is not really knowledge, it is a lie.

Apart from this, knowledge can be prayed for as in the case of Solomon, whom God appeared to and said, *"Ask what I shall give thee,"* and Solomon asked for wisdom and knowledge.

(2 Chron. 1:7) Therefore one of the ways to receive knowledge from God is to ask for it. *If any of you lack wisdom, let him ask of God, that giveth to all men liberally, and upbraideth not; and it shall be given him.* (James 1:5) Not only so but the word of God states that *the entrance of thy words giveth light.* (Psalms 119:130)

There is abundance of light and knowledge available to man if he is willing to accept it. This knowledge is true knowledge and with it comes peace, joy, and assurance, but there is just one catch. You must be willing to have a negative view of yourself. That's it! You must condemn yourself and justify the Lord Jesus Christ, and oh how man rebels at that! No that is not the knowledge he wants. So he turns his head and heart and tries to look in other places.

Knowledge From Man

There is knowledge to be gained from man. This is the scientific experiments and the personal lessons of life learned by individuals over the ages. Libraries and schools are places man can go to for knowledge about various things. Mainly this knowledge has to do with survival in this world: how to build guns, houses, farming, storage of food, medicine etc., how to treat disease, or how to operate on the human body. This knowledge is not wrong as long as it remains in the physical realm, or if it does not contradict the word of God.

This is man's knowledge and it is needed for the day-to-day physical struggles of life.

It has been said that necessity is the mother of invention and over the six thousand years of man's existence he has invented devices for survival, security and pleasure. The source of this knowledge is good as well.

Knowledge From Satan

There is another source of knowledge that is forbidden by God, and that is to seek knowledge from Satan. This knowledge is different from the first two. Yes, The Lord Jesus Christ has all knowledge. As a preacher once said, "Did it ever occur to you, that nothing ever occurred to God?" The Bible says, *"God...knoweth all things."* (1John 3:20) But God does not reveal all knowledge to us for we would not be able to handle it if He did.

It is like a small child that comes to his father and asks, "Daddy, what are you doing?" Children are so curious. The father tries to tell him, and then comes the long string of Why's. It's more than the young child can handle, but he knows his daddy knows what he is doing. So too, it is with us. God could not reveal all to us, for we would not be able to handle it, but one day we shall know even as we are known. Then we will have that knowledge, and all mysteries will be made known.

In this life though there remains the desire to know. Along with the desire is the assumption that if I could only know, then I could control tomorrow, or at least I would not be caught by surprise. You see, that removes faith, and without faith it is impossible to please God.

But this knowledge is only gained from a forbidden source, and through a forbidden means. This knowledge is also laced with lies. Much of it is true, but only enough to deceive the individual into a departure from the faith. *Now the Spirit speaketh expressly, that in the latter times some shall depart from the faith, giving heed to seducing spirits, and doctrines of devils.* (1 Tim. 4:1) Or there is just enough lies mixed in so as to be a barrier to union with the God of the universe, the Lord Jesus Christ.

The knowledge from Satan is a hidden knowledge. All that God wants you to know is readily open to you in the Word of God, and all that God will allow you to learn is readily open to you from man, but the knowledge Satan has for you is not readily open. It must be revealed supernaturally, or mystically. This is what is termed "divination," which is forbidden by God.

> *When thou art come into the land which the LORD thy God giveth thee,* ***thou shalt not learn to do after the abominations of those nations****.*
>
> *There shall not be found among you any one that maketh his son or his daughter to pass through the fire, or* ***that useth divination, or an observer of times, or an***

> ***enchanter, or a witch, Or a charmer, or a consulter with familiar spirits, or a wizard, or a necromancer.*** (Deuteronomy 18:9-11)

In the New Testament it is referred to as *"curious arts."* (Acts 19:19) And there are a number of reasons why it is called this.

For one, if you are not satisfied with the knowledge you have gained from the first two sources, that being God and man, then you will be curious to find more knowledge. This is sin, for when you have done all you can do physically, and all that you can do Spiritually by the word of God and prayer, and then you are to rest in the Lord Jesus Christ. This takes faith, and faith pleases God, for the Bible states that, *"Without faith it is impossible to please Him."* (Heb 11:6)

You KNOW that the Lord Jesus Christ knows exactly what is wrong, or let me say that He knows all of the unknowns. And when I write, "all" I mean, "all!" The Lord Jesus Christ knows all about you, your body, and tomorrow. You are to rest in Him.

> *Wherefore, if God so clothe the grass of the field, which to day is, and to morrow is cast into the oven, shall he not much more clothe you, O ye of little faith? Therefore take no thought, saying, What shall we eat? or, What shall we drink? or, Wherewithal shall we be clothed? (For after all these*

> *things do the Gentiles seek:) for your heavenly Father knoweth that ye have need of all these things. But seek ye first the kingdom of God, and his righteousness; and all these things shall be added unto you. Take therefore no thought for the morrow: for the morrow shall take thought for the things of itself. Sufficient unto the day is the evil thereof.* (Matthew 6:30-34)

You are to rest in the Lord Jesus Christ, but the problem comes when people will not rest in the Lord. For instance when a doctor has run tests, but still does not know what is wrong. You have prayed and searched the word of God, and you have read articles and books on your problem, yet still, you have no answer. So inside you, instead of resting in the Lord, your *curiosity* drives you on. You have got to find an answer, or a solution. It is here that you become vulnerable and tempted to go to forbidden means to find out forbidden knowledge, or at least in a forbidden way.

This knowledge is hidden from you, but through your *curiosity* you seek a means to find out this knowledge, when you ought instead to rest in the Lord Jesus Christ. There is a time to rest and a time to seek, though the seeking must be with God's approval.

It is the new age medicine that is often used to satisfy a *curious* mind that seeks answers to questions of life, death and the unknown. It has been said that, "Curiosity killed the cat." There comes a time when you are to trust and rest in the Lord Jesus Christ.

~

Don't Know How It Works

Another reason it is called curious arts is because when you use New Age medicine you never really know how it works. In the "art" of muscle testing, they have no idea how it works or why it works, all they know is that it works. Notice the following quotes:

Dr. Devi Nambudripad on vital energy:

> *No one knows how or why the vital energy gets into the body or how, when or where it goes when it leaves.* (Devi S. Nambudripad, Say Good-Bye To Illness, Buena Park, California, Delta Publishing Company, 2002, P. 125).

Dr. Robert Frost:

> *In Applied Kinesiology, as in any science, phenomena are encountered for which no current explanation exists.* (Robert Frost, Applied Kinesiology, Berkeley, California, North Atlantic Books, 2002, P. 12).

> *...Within the generally accepted medical model, many of the observed phenomena of AK (Applied Kinesiology) simply cannot be explained...Examiners using AK*

often test subtle energy substances such as homeopathic remedies, Bach Flower Remedies and gemstones held in the hand. An explanation of how the above methods could function does not exist within the models of classical medicine. (Robert Frost, Applied Kinesiology, Berkeley, California, North Atlantic Books, 2002, P. 43).

Touch for Health works with the subtle body energies...When we have a tool that can image the energetic cause of disease using this same computer programming, we will be closer to explaining what it is that Touch for Health does and how it works.

Dr. Bruce A.J. Dewe: In the mean time, we have, in Touch for Health, a tool for working with the connection between the mind and body, using the electromagnetic energy system known as "meridians," which interface the physical and subtle energy bodies. I have taken the liberty of redefining Touch for Health as the "science of energy balancing," for this is what **I believe we are doing. Technology to prove this will catch up eventually**. *We, however, need not wait for that to happen. The* **results** *of Touch for Health balancing are daily seen worldwide in 37 countries and many languages.* (John Thie, D.C. & Matthew Thie,

> Touch For Health, Camarillo, California, DeVorss & Co., 2007, Quote from trustee for Touch for Health, Dr. Bruce A.J. Dewe, P. iii-iv).

You can see by these few quotes that they do not know for sure what they are doing, or how they are doing it. They know what they are trying to do, and certain methods are producing reproducible results, but that is all they know. As Dr. Dewe said, *"The results...are daily seen worldwide."* In the practice of Acupuncture they have studied Qi (pronounced "chee") for 5,000 years and still they state they do not know what it is. All they know is that it works.

You see, it is curious. Whether it is NAET: Nambudripads' Allergy Elimination Technique, Touch for Health, Lepore Method, CRA: Contact Reflex Analysis, or any other method of muscle testing, the bottom line is that they do not know the nature of the phenomena, nor how it works. All they can say is that it does. It is a curious thing, a *curious art.*

Yes, there are many scientific sounding explanations as to how it works, but this is merely science falsely so called.

> *O Timothy, keep that which is committed to thy trust, avoiding profane and vain babblings, and oppositions of science falsely so called: Which some professing have erred concerning the faith.* (1 Timothy 6:20-21)

It is science falsely so called that will cause you to err from the faith. Muscle testing has yet to be proven scientifically, which would mean that it would have to operate in the physical realm. The truth is though that it is metaphysical in nature. Muscle testing operates outside the physical realm; therefore they will never be able to fully explain it with true science.

There are explanations coming from the chaos theory, and quantum physics, but chaos is a theory in and of itself, and quantum physics is a guessing game. Neither of these two are true science either. Muscle testing is what the bible calls a *curious art.* Study it, as much as you dare, you will never figure out exactly what it is, scientifically that is. Delve into the metaphysical realm and it won't take long to see exactly what it is. It is witchcraft!

This brings us to one very widely used method of divination in the New Age medicinal movement and it is the divination method of muscle testing. The other method that we will cover later is called "iridology" but for now we will explain muscle testing.

In the 1960's there was a Chiropractor by the name of Dr. George Goodheart. He was a Detroit Chiropractor and was seeking to help his patients by any means he could. Over time he incorporated a number of different disciplines of medicine into his chiropractic practice, one of which was manual muscle testing. Along with this he also incorporated the meridians of acupuncture, which we will discuss in more detail later.

His method of treatment became known as Applied Kinesiology. Kinesiology is the scientific study of movement, but Dr. Goodhearts' version is not to be confused with the true Kinesiology or biomechanics. True Kinesiology would be practices, or therapies used by physical therapists as they message and work the human body. This is a true scientific physical therapy. Applied Kinesiology is not the same as the true science found in medical hospitals and physical therapy offices. Applied Kinesiology is metaphysical in nature.

Applied Kinesiology is an integrated medicine. Dr. Goodheart incorporated western physical practices, such as deep tissue message and chiropractic adjustments with eastern mystical treatments such as meridian therapy and muscle testing.

Dr. Goodhearts' own statements about Applied Kinesiology show that even he believed that what he was doing was accessing a force that filled the universe to make a proper diagnosis, in other words, to reveal hidden knowledge about a person's health and body. In the preface, written by Dr. George Goodheart, of the book, Applied Kinesiology, by Robert Frost, it reads:

> *The body heals itself in a sure, sensible, practical, reasonable, and observable manner. "The healer within" can be approached from without. Man possesses a potential for recovery through the innate*

> *intelligence or the physiological homeostasis of the human structure.*
>
> *This benefits mankind individually and collectively. It benefits the doctor who has rendered the service, and it allows* ***the force which created the structure*** *to operate unimpeded.* (Robert Frost, Applied Kinesiology, Berkeley, California, North Atlantic Books, 2002, P. x).

This is an amazing and very revealing quote, as well as it shows how opposite of the word of God Applied Kinesiology is.

First of all you will notice that the founder of Applied Kinesiology refers to the *"innate intelligence."* The Innate Intelligence is a term that was widely used by a man by the name of D.D. Palmer and he was the founder of Chiropractic treatment. So to find out what Dr. Goodheart is referring to we will see what D.D. Palmer taught about this Innate Intelligence.

Journal of Canadian Chiropractic Association, article "DD Palmer and Innate Intelligence,"

> *"... a segment of that Intelligence which fills the universe, this universe, all wise, is metamerized, divided into metemeres as needed by individual being." Palmer felt that Innate had always existed. It is distinct and separate from the soul and bonds with the body at the moment of birth with the first breath of life. The fetus thus has no innate of its own, but*

must rely on the mother's during its early development. (Donahue J., DD Palmer and Innate Intelligence: Development, Division and Derision, Assoc Hist Chir, 1986, Quoted from the Journal of the Canadian Chiropractic Association, 1998; Vol. 42(1), P. 38)

Palmer further saw Innate as a dual entity, having both a physical and a spiritual part, but was considered as still being separate from the mind. Innate was eternal, while the mind existed only during life. Further, Innate's attributes were dispensed and directed through the body via the sympathetic nervous system. (Donahue J., DD Palmer and Innate Intelligence: Development, Division and Derision, Assoc Hist Chir, 1986, Quoted from the Journal of the Canadian Chiropractic Association, 1998; Vol. 42(1), P. 38)

By 1906 he had introduced Innate Intelligence as a distinct personality inhabiting the body along with Educated Intelligence. This doctrine taught that 'two persons' both occupied the same body, unaware of each other. Innate inhabited all parts of the body and communicated with the body through nerve ganglia. Innate was somehow considered the superior of the two Intelligences. (Keating J, The Evolution of Palmer's Metaphors and Hypothesis, Philosophical Constructs for the Chiropractic Profession. 1992; 2:9-19, Quoted from the Journal of the Canadian Chiropractic Association, 1998; Vol. 42(1), P. 38)

> *His ideas had their origin in concepts derived from the folk medicine, mysticism and occult practices of his time.* (Haldeman S., Modern Developmants in the Principles and Practice of Chiropractic, ed. Haldeman S., 1979, New York: Appleton-Century-Crofts. 390, Quoted from the Journal of the Canadian Chiropractic Association, 1998; Vol. 42(1), P. 38)

Notice then D.D. Palmer's belief of Innate Intelligencc. Hc believed that a person, after their first breath, has two intelligences in their body, but that the Innate Intelligence was an eternal superior intelligence that filled the universe, and that it is "all wise." Why, that is HIS GOD! He is describing a deity, but it is a pagan deity. He is describing what is called Pantheism; God is in all and through all. There is no doubt that what he believed was contrary to the word of God.

Now, let me say this right here. Very few doctors believe the word of God, but the reason that this is important is because this deity, or force that created the structure, is what they claim they are using to treat patients with, even Western Doctors who might be atheists are different in that they do not claim to be using pagan mystical means for healing.

He also believed that this Innate Intelligence had its own personality, it was eternal, and that it was the superior of the two intelligences in man's body. He believed that Innate ran the vital force of the body.

This innate intelligence is similar to what is called the Akashic records in witchcraft.

> **Akashic Chronicle, Akashic Planes, Akashic records**—*From the Sanskrit* **akasha** *(primary substance). A higher ethereal plane where the records of all time are recorded.*
>
> *Edgar Cayce was able to access these Akashic Records while in trance and thereby make health assessments and diagnoses as well as comment upon past and future lives of individuals. Quoted from the glossary of* Essential Wicca. (Paul Tuite'an, Estelle Daniels, Essential Wicca, Berkeley, California, The Crossing Press, 2001, P. 313)

Edgar Casey obviously was filled with a devil when this happened, and the true records are found in the word of God:

> *And I saw the dead, small and great, stand before God; and the books were opened: and another book was opened, which is the book of life: and the dead were judged out of those things which were written in the books, according to their works.* (Revelation 20:12)

And also:

For ever, O LORD, thy word is settled in heaven. (Psalms 119:89)

This lie of these Akashic records is the same one Satan used on Eve when he lied to her and said that she would become as gods, knowing good and evil. It is this desire to know, this desire to discover the unknown that can get you into trouble. Eve fell into the trap and mankind has suffered ever since. Yes, Adam ate also, but he was not deceived as Eve was.

> *And Adam was not deceived, but the woman being deceived was in the transgression.* (1Tim. 2:14)

So now, let's get back to Dr. George Goodheart, the founder of Applied Kinesiology, which is also known as muscle testing. He personally states in the preface of the book, Applied Kinesiology that:

> ***"...the healer within"*** *can be approached from without. Man possesses a potential for recovery through the* ***innate intelligence.***"

Why, he is talking about a god! If you think I am exaggerating he states this:

> *...it allows* ***the force*** *which created the structure.* (Robert Frost, Applied Kinesiology, Berkeley, California, North Atlantic Books, 2002, P. x)

"The force?" Hello star wars! Hello pagan pantheism! Hello Eastern Religion! Hello Satan!

That "created the structure"? No, my Bible states that:

> *For by him* (Jesus Christ) *were all things created, that are in heaven, and that are in earth, visible and invisible, whether they be thrones, or dominions, or principalities, or powers: all things were created by him, and for him: And he is before all things, and by him all things consist.* (Colossians 1:16-17)

So we see that the founder of muscle testing believes he is using the "Innate Intelligence," that, according to him, fills the universe, has its own personality, that it is all wise, and therefore knows exactly what is wrong with your body. You might say it is divine. He believes that he is communicating with the eternal intelligence of the universe! His purpose for this communication is to learn of hidden knowledge. Ah yes! There it is, the hidden knowledge. This shows that muscle testing is divination.

But what is divination?

The root word is divine, which means emanating from God, or a god.

Merriam-Webster online dictionary:

> *1: the art or practice that seeks to foresee or foretell future events or discover hidden knowledge usually by the interpretation of omens or by the aid of supernatural powers.* (Merriam-Webster online dictionary, Merriam-Webster.com, http://www.merriam-webster.com/dictionary/divination, 8/26/2010)

According to Erin Dragonsong, who is a practicing Witch for the past 20 years, and the founder of the web site wicca-spirituality.com (a website that gets up to half a million hits a year, and growing):

> *Any action that attempts to solicit information directly from the Divine, through the use of interpretive tools. In other words, this is the practice of using specific methods and tools to hear the guidance of the Divine.* (Erin Dragonsong, "How Do We Define Divination?", Wicca-Spiriutality.com, http://www.wicca spirituality. com/divination.html, 8/26/2010)

Both definitions would fit exactly what Dr. George Goodheart did, and what Applied Kinesiology is all about. There is no doubt that muscle testing is divination.

> *Applied Kinesiology (AK) is usually listed among divination methods. But*

> **human bodies are very effective divination tools**, *and this technique allows us to access deep wisdom that the mind cannot attain.* (Erin Dragonsong, "Applied Kinesiology: Your Body As A Divination Tool", Wicca-Spirituality.com, http://www.wicca-spirituality.com/applied-kinesiology.html, 8/26/2010)

During the years Dr. Goodheart practiced and developed his medical disciplines he taught others how to treat patients as he did. Other Chiropractors were interested and studied under Dr. Goodheart. There are now Applied Kinesiology schools where it is taught.

One such student, who also became one of Dr. Goodheart's first workshop leaders, was a saved man by the name of Dr. John Thie. He learned from Dr. Goodheart and then formed his own version which he named Touch for Health. Again, muscle testing is the main method of diagnosis in this treatment. (John Thie, D.C. & Matthew Thie, Touch For Health, Camarillo, California, DeVorss & Co., 2007, P. I)

Some other versions of Applied Kinesiology are Contact Reflex Analysis, and the man that developed this was a man by the name of Dr. D. A. Versendaal. There is Nambudripad's Allergy Elimination Technique, or NAET for short, which is the one my wife was messed up by. There is also another called, The Ultimate Healing System by Dr. Donald Lepore. There are many other variations of Applied Kinesiology, but they all have one thing in common and that is that the major diagnostic tool they use is muscle testing, and it is divination.

Dr. Goodheart introduced the term muscle testing, but the term is a lie, for they are not testing a muscle at all. What they are doing is using a muscle to indicate a yes or no answer from the Innate Intelligence. They are using the human body as an Ouija board! It is not a muscle test, it is a communication with another Intelligence that when pressed they do not know what it is. All they know is that it works. The proper term for the test is "energy testing" which was coined by a woman by the name of Donna Eden. In her book "Energy Medicine" she states:

> *I prefer the term "energy test" to the more common term "muscle test" to emphasize that the objective of the test is to determine not the strength of a muscle but rather how the body's energies are flowing through it.* (Donna Eden, Energy Medicine, New York, New York, Penguin Group, 2008, P. 51)

The problem is that it is forbidden in the word of God.

Satan is the Master of deception. *Now the Serpent was more subtle than any beast of the field which the Lord God had made.* (Gen 3:1) The word subtle means so delicate or precise as to be difficult to discern. Yes, Satan is the Master at this.

He has bibles that look and sound like real bibles, but they are not the word of God, they are merely counterfeits. It is the King James 1611 that is the truly perfect and preserved word of God. If you don't believe me check it out for yourself. See what verses are left out of the new versions, and what words are changed. Check it out if you don't want to believe me, and I would not recommend you believing me anyway. You need to find out for yourself.

I'm telling you that Satan is very subtle, so you must look closely to see the deception. Again that is why it is so very, very important to have the very words of God. Satan has churches that look like real churches but they are counterfeit. Let's say you are an intellectual. Well, Satan has an intellectual church for you. Let's say you are emotional. Well, Satan has an emotional church for you. On and on it goes.

This is why at the very root of this whole study the final authority must be the inerrant words of God. I am not the final authority for I am a man that is writing this because I got messed up in these deceptions. What you had better do is find a copy of the inerrant words of the true God and compare everything with them. The only thing that will manifest error is the truth. What I think, and what you think doesn't amount to a hill of beans, as they say in the Carolina's. What matters is what God said!

So if Dr. Goodheart coined the term, "muscle testing" then what was it called before Dr. Goodheart showed up? By the way, muscle testing is listed in various places as a divination method so I am not the only one who is stating this. It's just that I am one of a few Christians who realize that it is a sin for anyone to practice muscle testing.

> *Dowsing, an ancient* ***method of divination*** *with a pendulum or other tool, is basically a form of* ***self-muscle testing*** *using a tool to exaggerate the body's response and make it more noticeable.* (Victoria Anisman-Reiner, "Manual Muscle Testing", naturalmedicine.suite101.com, http://naturalmedicine.suite101.com/article.cfm/manual-muscle-testing-a23265, 8/26/2010) Victoria Anisman-Reiner, B.Sc, C.C.A., is a writer, a teacher in holistic health and energy healing, and an aromatherapist.

> ***Systems of divination*** *using yes/no answers can serve as an interface for your communication with nature... Through the movement of a pendulum, you can determine a yes or no response. Many people erroneously assume that it is the pendulum itself that is giving a response to their question, when in actuality* ***the pendulum is a method of divination*** *that interfaces with other spirits...You can use it to connect to your higher self, the ascended masters, angels, and faery nature spirits and devas...* ***Another method for communicating with nature is to use applied***

> ***kinesiology, or muscle testing**, to get yes/no answers through your body. Applied kinesiology is used to test the body for helpful or harmful substances, determining if a substance energetically strengthens or weakens the body. The same technique has been applied to spiritual communication...* (Christopher Penczak, Ascension Magick: Ritual, Myth & Healing for the New Aeon, Woodbury, Minnesota, Llewellyn Publications, 2007, P. 217-218)

> *However, like the California Essences which they resemble in scope and character, choice of the appropriate remedy relies on applied kinesiology or muscle testing, pendulum dowsing, other forms of **divination** and intuitive diagnosis.* (Helen Graham & Gregory Vlamis, Bach Flower Remedies for Animals, Tallahassee, Florida, Findhorn Press, 1st Indian Edition, 2002, P.18)

But again, what was it called before Dr. Goodheart came along? Well, the term for muscle testing is called "body dowsing." It is a form of Dowsing, which again, is an occult practice and form of divination. Some claim the difference from Dowsing and Divination is that Divination will also attempt to forecast the future, while dowsing only reveals what is or has been.

This may be a technical point but for this study both are used to reveal hidden knowledge through supernatural means and as such I will place dowsing in the same realm as divining. Notice now the following information about dowsing and Applied Kinesiology. This is quoted from a homeopathic website.

> *For centuries, healing systems have been using a form of a biofeedback system to diagnose illness and* ***discover hidden things.*** (There's divination: Revealing hidden knowledge through supernatural methods.) *Its constant elements, the tester and the instrument, are the same as in* ***applied kinesiology.*** *The pre-agreed upon response is a little different; it uses a impulse of movement rather than resistance to movement. That biofeedback system is* ***dowsing.*** (Doug Hoff, "medical dowsing", http://homeoinfo.com/08_non-classical_topics/dowsing/medical_dowsing.php,, 8/26/2010). (Bio: http://homeoinfo.com/me.php)
>
> Dowsing is a form of "clairvoyance" and has the same appeal to scientists as people who bend spoons. But people find water, **cure illness**, and solve mysteries with it. Dowsers use the most elaborate diagnostic systems with homeopathy today.
>
> *...Dowsers also use the deltoid muscle group, as well as wrist and other muscles, to facilitate a response as in kinesiology.* ***Other dowsers***

> ***even use resistance to a muscle group exactly like muscle testers.*** (Doug Hoff, "medical dowsing", http://homeoinfo.com/08_non-classical_topics/dowsing/medical_dowsing.php,, 8/26/2010). (Bio: http://homeoinfo.com/me.php)

Do you see what you are dealing with? Applied Kinesiology is the metaphysical practice of body dowsing, and it is witchcraft plain and simple. Did you know that Witchcraft is a work of the flesh as listed in Galatians 5, which, by the way, is written to Christians?

> *Now the works of the flesh are manifest, which are these; Adultery, fornication, uncleanness, lasciviousness, 20 Idolatry,* ***witchcraft****, hatred, variance, emulations, wrath, strife, seditions, heresies, 21 Envyings, murders, drunkenness, revellings, and such like: of the which I tell you before, as I have also told you in time past, that they which do such things shall not inherit the kingdom of God.* (Galatians 5:19-21)

You'll loose your inheritance! That is a reference to the millennial reign with Jesus Christ.

There is more from the same author:

> *The Ouija board user assumes that his arm movements are spiritually controlled but are first of all controlled*

> *by commands from his brain.* ***The Ouija board and kinesiology are in the same group of diagnostic devices because of the psychic element****. (Emphasis added) Unfortunately, the Ouija board is not known for its diagnostic capability. It was too successful as a popular parlor game.* (Doug Hoff, "medical dowsing", http://homeoinfo.com/08_non-classical_topics/dowsing/medical_dowsing.php,, 8/26/2010). (Bio: http://homeoinfo.com/me.php)

Hello! There is a psychic element, according to this author, to muscle testing, Applied Kinesiology, dowsing, etc. You are dealing with elements of witchcraft plain and simple.

Dowsing and Applied Kinesiology are one and the same. To be specific it is body dowsing, which is a practice that goes back over 4,000 years. It is an occult practice and only one form of dowsing. There are many other forms of dowsing such as using the pendulum, L-rods, switches from trees and others. It is all supernaturally done. Over and over the authors of articles on dowsing state that though it is a practice that has been done for thousands of years, yet they still do not know exactly how or why it works. All they know is that it does.

Dowsing is mentioned in the word of God, yet when it is, dowsing is condemned.

> *My people* ***ask counsel at their stocks, and their staff***

> ***declareth unto them****: for the spirit of whoredoms hath caused them to err, and they have gone a whoring from under their God.* (Hosea 4:12)

"And their staff declareth..." Here is a staff that can declare things, and in dowsing there is a communication that takes place for it is the sole reason for the dowsing in the first place. This is no different than body dowsing, or muscle testing. All of it is divination and it is condemned in the word of God.

Iridology

But muscle testing is only one form of divination that is commonly used today in the New Age health field, and that is also commonly used by many Christians. The other commonly used form of divination that is being used by Christians is what is known as Iridology.

> *'There is nothing new under the sun.' This proverbial saying from Ecclesiastes is certainly justified as far as iris diagnosis is concerned. Historically, iris diagnosis, like acupuncture, goes back to ancient Chinese methods of healing. Both methods are associated with astrology.* (Kurt E. Koch, Occult ABC, Grand Rapids, Michigan, Kregel Publications, 1986, P. 100)

Iridology is also listed as a form of divination in the paranormal dictionary as well as other encyclopedic libraries. Iridology also goes back thousands of years and is the art of scrying the iris of the eye to determine health issues in the body. It is in the same category as muscle testing.

> *Rayid enables the harmonious integration of masculine and feminine energy. Like a full solar eclipse, in which the Sun and Moon are perfectly aligned with the Earth, the Rayid Method of Iris Interpretation honors the presence of light flowing through the sacred union of a man and woman.* (Denny Ray Johnson, What The Eye Reveals, Boulder, Rayid Publications, 1995, Inside Cover)

Notice from the previous quote the use of light. This is, in the classical sense, the occult practice of scrying, which is reading the light through a translucent object. In the word of God it states that the eye twinkles. "*... In the twinkling of an eye...*" (1 Cor. 15:52). This twinkling has to do with its light. *Now Eli was ninety and eight years old; and his eyes were dim, that he could not see.* (1Sam. 4:15) When the eyes grow weak they dim.

> *The forgoing facts presented on the subject of muscle testing, involves the amazing neural communications system within the body* ***as with iridology****.* (Guy Danowski, http://www.

> betterhealththruresearch.com/Biokinesiology.htm)
>
> *Furthermore, homeopathy is related to acupuncture, auriculotherapy, **iridology** and the practice of hypnotists. Now, all these methods are occult or very suspect of such influence.* (H. J. Bopp, M.D., "Homeopathy Examined", Logos Resource Pages, http://logosresourcepages.org/NewAge/homeopat.htm, 8/26/2010)

I had one man email me and state that when he was a young man growing up, his family would go to the doctor and the doctor would look into his eyes, and I too remember having a doctor look into, and examine my eyes. But that is not what is happening when you go to an Iridologist. Iridologists do not look into your eyes; they specifically look **on** the iris of your eye. That is much different than looking into the eyeball to examine the physical workings thereof. For that matter Iridologists do not even look **into** your eye.

What they do is called in the occult world, scrying. Scrying is the art of peering into a translucent object and divining by reading the light in the object. This takes the form of reading crystal balls, crystals, water in a bowl, and also the eye, as in iridology.

Iridology has been debunked many times and proven to be unscientific.

> *There have been five reviews published in medical journals*

> *reporting various scientific tests of iridology (Berggren, 1985; Cockburn, 1981; Worrall, 1984, 1985; Knipschild, 1988; Simon, Worthen, and Mitas, 1979), and they all dismiss iridology as a medical fraud. In particular, the review by Berggren (1985) concludes: "Good care of patients is inconsistent with deceptive methods, and iridology should be regarded as a medical fraud."* (Berggren, L. (1985) "Iridology: A critical review". Acta Ophthalmologica 63(1): 1-8. University of Cambridge, http://www.cl.cam.ac.uk/~jgd1000/iridology.html, 8/26/2010)

An Iridologist will look at the iris of the eye and then compare his findings to a chart of the iris, also known as an iris key. I have had many people assume that there is only one chart, but this is not true.

> *...Karl Schulte, a very well-known iris diagnostician, mentions in his Encyclopedia of Iris Diagnosis, sixteen ways of dividing the iris. Another expert speaks of nineteen iris keys. The different systems cannot be harmonized.* (Kurt E. Koch, Occult ABC, Grand Rapids, Michigan, Kregel Publications, 1986, P. 102)

As you can see, many tests have been done to see if there is any validity in the curious art of iridology, and every time the test has revealed that it does not hold up to true science. So often I have read where it is listed as quack medicine, or a medical hoax, but it is a mistake to do that. You see there is a difference when iridology is tested in a clinical scientific setting, or when it is practiced in an office. You see, how do you explain the fact that it works?

There is no doubt that iridologists, as well as muscle testers, can diagnose health problems, sometimes with 100% accuracy. What is the difference from the cold clinical setting and the office? Well, the difference is in the office there is a familiar spirit present that is guiding the examination. That familiar spirit is communicating with the doctor and revealing to him or her what is going on in the patient's body.

> *Medieval ophthalmoscopy, or the prophesying of character from the appearance of a person's eyes is on a level with chiromancy, the art of fortunetelling by means of the lines on the hand; metoposcopy, the art of interpreting the lines on the forehead: and physiognomy, the art of interpreting the features, warts, and spots on the face'*
>
> *...There are psychic, occult methods of diagnosis. In order not to give rise to any misunderstandings, I must say that there are few occult iris diagnosticians. Many iris diagnosticians have nothing to*

> *do with the occult... The medical value of the diagnosis, however, is extraordinarily thin. In many cases it is meaningless.*
>
> *It is a different case with those iris diagnosticians who work by occult means. They usually produce 100 percent accurate diagnosis.* (Kurt E. Koch, Occult ABC, Grand Rapids, Michigan, Kregel Publications, 1986, P. 102-103)

Again, it is a form of divination for they are revealing hidden truth through supernatural means.

Bernard Jensen is the leading Doctor of Iridology in the United States. In his book "Iridology Simplified", he states:

> *It (Iridology) is the kind of science that cannot be related through scientific tests, for it does not provide clinical information.*
>
> *The scientific explanation of exactly how this process works neurologically is still forthcoming.* (Bernard Jensen, Iridology Simplified, Escondito, California, Iridologists International, 1980, P. 1,4)

As with all vitalistic medical systems, when it comes to true scientific evidence to show how it works, or even if it can be proven that it does work, there is little to none. All they can do is point to the results and say, see it works. What we know is that it works and science is just going to have to catch up to us. We are far ahead of science.

No, that is not true. You are not far ahead of science; you are just outside the realm of science. What you are into is science falsely so called: you are in to the metaphysical realm, which is outside physical science.

This is not to say that it does not work, for it does. It's just that what makes it work is Occult in nature and wrong.

For more evidence notice its companionship with Chinese medicine, which was born out of Taoism.

Quoted from: Iridology: A Practical Guide To Iris Analysis, Adam Jackson:

> *I was absolutely amazed to notice how the iris chart correlates to the Chinese findings, but I have since found these correlation's to be more and more frequent in the field of natural medicine.*
>
> *As far as the sheng cycle is concerned, there is little doubt in my mind that it helps us to have a more holistic view of the iris, by giving us a better understanding of the possible causes and effects of disease and therefore the most appropriate and effective remedies.* (Adam J. Jackson, Iridology: A Practical Guide To Iris Analysis, London, Vermillion Press, 1992, P. 81)

We will study much on the Chinese systems later in this book. But it does not take much to see that the origin of the Chinese medicine is metaphysical and wrong. Its philosophy is also based on vitalism, nature/earth worship and Astrology. Iridology, as with all of the New Age medicine has its own philosophy and beliefs, and these are spiritual at their core, thus the term metaphysical or occult. It is outside the realm of the physical.

The following definition is quoted from a glossary from a book entitled, Essential Wicca:

> **Metaphysics** *-More 'politically correct' term for what used to be called 'occult.' The study of the relationships between underlying reality and its manifestations. Psychic studies and related disciplines.* (Paul Tuite'an, Estelle Daniels, Essential Wicca, Berkeley, California, The Crossing Press, 2001, P. 383)

Notice the following quote from one of, if not the leading iridologist in America, Bernard Jensen.

> *It [The Brain] then relays information easily to the iris using the optic nerve as its path."*
>
> *"To understand what is showing up in the iris, you will need to learn iridology's language and philosophy.*
>
> *You will need these tools to understand manifestations that cannot*

> *be explained by the terminology, philosophy, and current understanding of orthodox medicine.*
>
> *Iridology is based on the principles of reflexology.* (Bernard Jensen & Donald V. Bodeen, Visions Of Health: Understanding Iridology, New York, Avery Publishers, 1988, P. 56)

Reflexology is often claimed to have originated in Egypt, while others claim it is Chinese in origin and a form of Acupuncture. Personally I would agree with the latter as Reflexology works by energetic channels just as Acupuncture. These channels are said to effect zones. As I will cover in the next chapter, if you are practicing traditional Chinese medicine then you are working with spirit medicine. It is not true science, it is the *"science falsely so called"* spoken of in 1 Timothy 6:20.

If Iridology is associated, or can work in conjunction with Traditional Chinese medicine then there is no doubt that Iridology is contrary to the word of God and metaphysical at its core. A Christian should keep far, far away or they may end up quenching the Spirit of God in their body.

Dr. Jensen again, from his journal, Iridologists International:

> *There is much to be said in the development today concerning the ancient knowledge of the zone meridians in the body. While we are familiar with the terms Acupuncture, Reflexology, and so forth, new names are appearing*

such as Touch for Health, Kinesiology, MST (Muscle Structure Test), and others. (Bernard Jensen, Iridologists International, Volume 2, Number 7, P. 4)

In Spring 1988, we received an invitation to teach our work in Iridology and Nutrition in Taiwan. The Chinese government wanted us to teach at their 2,700 bed Veteran's General Hospital in Taiwan in conjunction with the Oriental Medical School of Traditional Medicine . . . The interest shown in this class was so great that they incorporated our teachings to use along with acupuncture, moxibustion, and herbology in their regular hospital services. (Bernard Jensen, Iridologists International, Volume 4, Number 1, P. 7,8)

These last quotes I included to show Iridology's association with Traditional Chinese medicine, for it is this medicine that is foundational in much of the holistic medicine today. Just the very fact that it is Chinese should make the Christian skeptical at the start. The origin is obviously Satanic in that it originated from pagan religion.

Using metaphysical medicine and thus occult medicine opens one up to unclean spiritual influences. You may end up paying a price far greater than you expected. Consider the following story:

Example 104 A young man went to an iris diagnostician. Not only was

> *he told what his illness was, but he was told the future. The young man recovered, but as far as his faith was concerned, he displayed remarkable changes. He began to feel physical pain when he went to church or when he wanted to read the Bible at home. He lost the ability and desire to pray or to sing Christian hymns. At the same time, personality defects appeared. He became an addict, a chain-smoker, and depressions set in which led to a complete emotional breakdown. His organic healing was dearly paid for in terms of emotional complications. This eye diagnostician works in an area known for its many occult healers.* (Kurt E. Koch, Occult ABC, Grand Rapids, Michigan, Kregel Publications, 1986, pg 104)

As I studied Applied Kinesiology, also known as muscle testing, it became clear that it is not biblical at all. It is an occult practice known as body dowsing which is a form of divination. Along with it is also Iridology, which is another form of divination, and is associated with Eastern medicine.

One time there was a king. This king was in charge of a great army of soldiers who were fighting for the Lord their God. The problem was that this king had been disobedient to his God and therefore was not getting messages from his God.

Before him the enemy gathered and a fear ran through his soul that made him shiver to the bones. Over and over, in vain he tried to contact his God for light as to what to do and how to fight the battle, yet all he received was silence. Urim and Thumin did not work. The dreams did not work. His heart was not right and he would not repent. With the battle approaching ever nearer he began to panic.

Sending a couple of men out he commanded them to go find a woman with a familiar spirit, also known as a witch. The men hurried out and after a short time returned with knowledge that there was a witch not far away in Endor.

The king and a couple of his men immediately left to go to the woman, the witch, in Endor. Upon arrival at her house he quickly entered in and asked her to bring up a dead man whose name was Samuel. As she began to contact the dead, sure enough Samuel came up which terrified the witch.

The king asked Samuel if there was any news and Samuel told him that the king and his sons would be with him tomorrow. Fear now gripped the king and he almost passed out but was encouraged by the witch and his men to eat some food, which he finally did after much urging.

The next day though, while in battle he died and the Lord said this about him,

> *So Saul died for his transgression which he committed against the LORD, even against the word of the*

> *LORD, which he kept not, and also for asking counsel of one that had a familiar spirit, to inquire of it;*
>
> *And inquired not of the LORD: therefore he slew him, and turned the kingdom unto David the son of Jesse.*
>
> (1Chr. 10:13-14)

Saul had used divination, and yes, he received truthful hidden knowledge, but it was sin and God killed him. That is what God thinks of divination!

Chapter

3

ENERGY OR BLOOD

There is a desire in most people to want to help others get well. Usually if you have a problem and tell others about it you will end up with recommendations on how to get better, or to be cured of your problem. When my voice was going out, people constantly were giving me "remedies" for my voice. They meant well and were trying to help.

There is a certain satisfaction that comes from knowing that you have helped someone get better, or healed, or relieved of his or her pain. Oh sure, there are those who could care less, but most people will readily offer suggestions as an attempt to help others feel better.

Wouldn't it be frustrating to be a doctor, or anyone for that matter, and diagnose a problem but have no idea how to cure it? I'm sure there are many doctors who diagnose sickness and then tell the patient, "there is nothing I can do." I'm sure those doctors have a certain sense of frustration for they desire to help their patients and yet are limited to what they can do.

I remember the story of a young man, though old enough to drink. In his soul he knew things were not right between him and God. He knew that he was headed for Hell. At times he would be outside with his friends and as they were laughing and partying he would wander off and listen to the birds. With curiosity his friends would ask him what he was doing? He would be in a kind of daze and again they would ask what he was doing? He then would reply, "When we get there you won't remember these sounds and things, but I will." He was collecting memories for Hell.

As he sat at a bar one night he began to talk to himself out loud, "Sam, you're going to Hell, what are you going to do? I don't want to go to Hell but what can I do? God, it's not your fault, I know." You see, he diagnosed the problem but didn't have the solution. Not too long after that he heard about how God, the Lord Jesus Christ, had died for him on the cross and paid for his sins. He then asked Jesus Christ to come into his heart and save him. He found the solution.

To diagnose a problem but not have a solution is a frustrating thing, and many doctors are in that position.

So far I have described a couple of divination techniques used in alternative medicine, which are muscle testing and iridology. Divination is the new age method of diagnosis, but what good is the diagnosis if you cannot prescribe a cure? The whole point of diagnosis is to determine what is needed to procure the cure.

Traditional medicine has many ways to diagnose sickness, but is limited at times to a cure. In these situations New Age medicine rides up on a white horse like a knight in shining armor to rescue the fair young maiden. New Age medicine claims to be able to cure any sickness there is, and if you think I am exaggerating, just look at the title of Dr. Devi Nambudripad's book which is: Say Good-Bye to Illness.

> *Wouldn't it be wonderful if allergy sufferers could be taught a simple test, which could detect and predetermine the potentially harmful reactions between substances and people before the adverse* ***electromagnetic energies*** *create havoc in their systems, bringing on ill health and unhappiness?*
>
> *You are now able to do just that. You can manipulate your brain and nervous systems as you desire and for your benefit* ***using Oriental medical principles****. You can reprogram your brain to accept incompatible energies as suitable ones and use them for your own benefit, rather than allow them to cause energy blockages and imbalances, and finally* **DISEASES***. It is not necessary to stay away from certain food items that you like or throw away your favorite clothes because they make you sick. You do not have to hide indoors during the pollen season or spend the rest of your days in metropolitan areas instead of vacationing in the mountains because of your fear of poison oak and mosquitos. You do*

not have to look pale, sick and aged instead of using the latest cosmetic products that would make you look at least 20 years younger because of your fear of skin rashes and hives. You do not have to hide from sunny beaches for fear of skin problems and skin cancers. You do not have to end up in divorce court **(Divorce is now a disease? My comment)** *a month after your marriage that you thought would last forever. You could even avoid seeing your teenagers using drugs and alcohol, some even ultimately ending up in suicides, if you are able to uncover the problems in time, before they take over their lives.*

Our psychiatric hospitals might be empty if the causes of the psychiatric patients' ***energy blockages*** *could be found and removed. Our county jails would not be packed if inmates' emotional allergies were tested and treated. Heart attacks and other tragic deaths due to cancer and other incurable diseases might be prevented if everyone in the world could be taught to find their* ***suitable electromagnetic fields****, stick to them, and avoid unsuitable energies from a very early age.* ***NAET could be used to change the unsuitable***

> ***energies into suitable ones.*** *If everyone learned and practiced these techniques from childhood on, it might be possible to stop many disease processes, perhaps even delay the aging process.* (Devi S. Nambudripad, Say Good-Bye To Illness, Buena Park, California, Delta Publishing Company, 2002, P. 27-28)

New Age medicine claims to have the answer and cure for any sickness you have. For them the cure is "energy." You see, New Age medicine claims that all sickness originates from the same source and that is an imbalance in your energy. The Bible claims that all sickness originated from sin when Adam and Eve disobeyed God and partook of the tree of the knowledge of good and evil. (Genesis 3:6)

At the root of the New Age Medicine is a belief in a universal life force. The term for this belief is "Vitalism." This unbiblical belief is defined as:

> *...a doctrine that the functions of a living organism are due to a vital principle distinct from physicochemical forces.* (1, Vitalism, P Gove, Editor, Webster's Third New World Dictionary, Springfield, Merriam-Webster Inc., 1993, P. 2558)

Then vitalism is outside the physical thus making it meta-physical, otherwise known as occult.

This is foundational to the New Age Medicine. This vital life force is what the holistic doctors are preoccupied with. It is their whole focus in terms of how they treat an individual. The vital life force has many names, and I have read that there are over 90 names for it. Yet, with all of these people studying this life force and naming it what they think it is, still to this day they do not know, nor can they for sure tell anyone what it is.

As for the names of this "force" that is supposedly at the heart of all life, D.D. Palmer has called it the "Innate Intelligence."

> *To the Hindus it is called prana, to the Chinese qi, to the Japanese ki, and to the Hawaiians Mana. Hippocrates referred to it as Vis Medicatrix Naturae. Galen called it Pneuma.* (Guiley R., Universal life force, Encyclopedia of Mystical and Paranormal Experience. San Francisco, Harper, 1991, P. 626-630, Quoted from the Journal of the Canadian Chiropractic Association 1998; vol. 42(1) P. 36)

> *Central to Taoist world-view and practice is qi (chi). Qi is life-force – that which animates the forms of the world. It is the vibratory nature of phenomena – the flow and tremoring that is happening continuously at molecular, atomic and sub-atomic levels. In Japan it is called "ki," and in India, "prana" or "shakti." The ancient Egyptians referred to it as "ka," and the ancient Greeks as "pneuma." For Native Americans it is the "Great*

> *Spirit" and for Christians, the "Holy Spirit." In Africa it's known as "ashe" and in Hawaii as "ha" or "mana."* (Elizabeth Reninger, "What Is Qi (Chi)?", About.com, http://taoism.about.com/od/qi/a/Qi.htm, 1/21/2010)

With all due respect to Dr. Reninger, she is wrong and it is a lie to claim that the Holy Spirit is the same as Qi, Ki, or Prana. That is a blasphemous statement for all of the other names are names given to an unclean spirit, or spirits. This is not hard to show for as we get into Acupuncture, for example, you will see that the energy, or Qi, they are working with, runs in the flesh. The apostle Paul in the word of God states, *"I know that in me, that is in my flesh, dwelleth no good thing."* (Romans 7:18) This force that runs in the flesh is not a good thing, and it is contrary to the word of God.

This vitalistic belief goes back many thousands of years for it is at the heart of Taoist and Hindu beliefs as well as others. But it is contrary to the word of God for it is stated in the word of God:

> *God, who at sundry times and in divers manners spake in time past unto the fathers by the prophets, Hath in these last days spoken unto us by his Son, whom he hath appointed heir of all things, by whom also he made the worlds; Who being the brightness of his glory, and the express image of his person, and* ***upholding all***

things by the word of his power.
(Hebrews 1:1-3)

According to the word of God, you, as well as everything else in this creation, are *"upheld by the word of His power."* In other words Jesus Christ is what holds you together. *"And he is before all things, and by him all things consist."* (Colossians 1:17)

From the beginning to this present time Jesus Christ is what holds all things together. One of these days though, the word of God states that this whole universe is going to be *dissolved... and melt with fervent heat.* (2 Pet. 3:10-12) After that there is going to be a judgment; it's called the great white throne judgment, and the lost, among others, are going to stand before God and give account of the things they did in this life. They will be judged according to their works.

Can you picture a great white throne, and it is a *very great* throne, for the word of God states that Heaven is God's throne, and earth is his footstool. That is a mighty big throne. On that throne is the God of the universe who knows everything you have ever done, said, or even thought, and it all has been recorded in books. The Bible says that, *"it is appointed unto man once to die, but after this the judgment."* (Heb. 9:27) One day you are going to stand before God.

As the souls stand and give account, what are they standing on? The Heaven and the earth have fled away and are dissolved. The souls are suspended on nothing. They walk; they stand; they are judged; yet they are merely standing on nothing. Below them is a roar, and a smell that emanates from a lake the Bible calls a lake of fire. As they look at the throne, and then look down below their feet, perhaps the thought will finally get through to them that the only thing holding them up is the One on that throne.

Ah yes! Some people get that through their heads in this life and get born again, but for others it will be far too late when that truth sinks into their thick skull. You must realize today that God himself holds you together. He is the power and the force that runs the universe. He holds all things together and even has your breath in his hand.

What these poor, depraved New Age sinners are trying to do is understand the power of God apart from God Himself and it can't be done. I say they are trying to study and understand the power of God, but due to their spiritual blindness and biblical ignorance they don't realize that they have been given a counterfeit. The energy or force that they are working with is a Satanic counterfeit that has deceived them and preoccupied them for over 5,000 years so as to damn their souls and take them to Hell. Now you may think I am being a bit too hard, yet it doesn't take long to figure out what they are working with if you have the true Bible and believe it.

Energy, energy, energy: they study and work with energy. To them it is the "vital energy" which, in their mind, is the source of health and life. This "Qi", which Hippocrates referred to it as "Vis Medicatrix Naturae". There are so many names for it, yet they do not know what it is.

> *As such, vitalism is considered a metaphysical doctrine.* (Beckner M. "Vitalism", The Encyclopedia of Philosophy, P. Edwards, Editor. 1967, The Macmillan Co: New York. p. 253-256. Quoted from the Journal of the Canadian Chiropractic Association, 1998, Volume 42(1), P. 36)

Then vitalism, this belief in a vital bio-energy that permeates the universe, is outside the realm of reality in that it seeks to explain an ultimate reality rather than what is apparent. So you are now entering the world, the realm, of the unexplainable. So rational explanations are not needed. What will matter is not how something works or does not. All that matters will be the results.

In philosophy this is known as "Pragmatism." Notice the warning given in the word of God, from the book, which has an emphasis towards the last group of Christians on the earth right before the Rapture. *Beware lest any man spoil you through philosophy and vain deceit, after the tradition of men, after the rudiments of the world, and not after Christ.* (Col. 2:8) Just because it works does not make it right!

Vitalism is also beyond the realm of true science. The Bible warns the Christian to, *"beware of oppositions of science falsely so called."* **1 Timothy 6:20, 1611 King James Bible: The New corrupt**

Bibles have removed the reference to science and merely call it knowledge falsely so called. The King James 1611 is the only Version that has the word "science" in it. Why is this important? Because even though vitalism is metaphysical in nature, yet when you begin to read all the books on this medicine they attempt to sound scientific. Applied Kinesiology, Homeopathy, Acupuncture, and others all attempt to sound scientific and in the end they are metaphysical. Just because some of them may be able to reproduce certain results, yet when they are pushed into a corner they cannot explain how or why they get the results. Often times though the results are not reproducible with reliability.

The main thing that is not explainable is the vitalistic energy. They believe that it is vital for life; they believe it is real, they communicate with an intelligence, but they do not know what that intelligence is.

At the foundation is "energy." As author, healer and lecturer Donna Eden entitled the first chapter of her book "Energy Medicine," "*Energy Is All There Is.*"

But what is energy? What does the Bible say about energy? What does the Bible say about energy healing? Should we not consult the Words of the Creator of the Universe?

In Dr. John Thie's book and manual, Touch for Health, for example it states:

> *Touch for Health works with the subtle body energies that are just*

beginning to be explained by quantum physics. Conventional Western medicine has made much progress, through the use of the CAT scan, PET and MRI scanners, to explain the physical and biochemical components of the human cellular body. When we have a tool that can image the ***energetic cause of disease*** *using this same computer programming, we will be closer to explaining what it is that Touch for Health does and how it works.*

In the meantime, we have, in Touch for Health, a tool for working with the connection between the mind and body, using the ***electromagnetic energy system known as "meridians,"*** *which interface the physical and subtle energy bodies. I have taken the liberty of redefining Touch for Health as the* ***"science of energy balancing,"*** *for this is what I believe we are doing. Technology to prove this will catch up eventually. We, however, need not wait for that to happen. The results of Touch for Health balancing are daily seen worldwide in 37 countries and many languages.* (John Thie, D.C. & Matthew Thie, Touch For Health, Camarillo, California, DeVorss & Co., 2007, P. iii-iv)

You see they do not know how it works, or why it works. In Acts 19:19 these satanic practices are called, ***"curious arts."*** (I say satanic because when they are repented of there is revival showing that it is wrong and from the Devil.) One of the reasons they are called "curious" is because you never know how they work. When I was muscle tested and felt the pulse of whatever go through my hand it caught my attention and made me curious as to what it was, but I never got an answer. At least not an absolute answer, and you never will get an absolute answer as to how any of this medicine works, for it is metaphysical, and therefore curious!

It is interesting to note that the Latin etymology of the word curious is "cura", or care, as in medical care! These curious arts have to do with medical care, also known as witchcraft. It is also associated with many books. If you go into a bookstore you will find many books on this subject, some of which are very expensive. It is these books that were burned in the book of Acts 19 when they had a revival.

I thought it so classic that when I preached on the subject of the dangers of New Age medicine showing that it was witchcraft after the service a visiting pastor made a comment to one of his friends that it seemed kind of strange to preach on a subject like that for a revival meeting. Hello? It was this subject and works that were repented of that brought forth revival in the word of God! Ding, Dong; Ding, Dong; anybody home???

The Energy

What is the energy of energy medicine? Again there are over 90 names for the energy and growing. There have been tests to determine what it is. Is it merely electricity? Or is it electrical in nature?

It seems that most will attribute some sort of electrical make up to it. They will use such names as electromagnetic, or bio-electric, or bio-energy, or magnetic and on and on they go, but no one can determine it for sure. Even the Chinese who have been working with Qi for 5,000 years state that it is all theory. They do not know what Qi is. All they can do is state what the results of it are.

Some have done electrical tests on the meridians of the body, and at the meridian points, with a special instrument that has an indicator on it such as a light. The light will turn on when it passes over the meridian point, and will go out when it is on other parts of the skin. From this they conclude that it must be electrical in nature.

Well, this may be a half-truth, but it is best to go to the word of God for the answer. You see, these people never go to the word of God for they ignore the word of God. The only author so far that I have read that has made a reference to the word of God is Dr. John Thie, for he was born again. He was messed up, but he was born again. He claims that the energy is the word of God from John 1:1-2. He is close to the truth, and yet he is so far away. I will explain this in a bit.

As far as this energy being electrical in nature notice what the word of God says:

> *12 Now a thing was secretly brought to me, and mine ear received a little thereof. 13 In thoughts from the visions of the night, when deep sleep falleth on men, 14 Fear came upon me, and trembling, which made all my bones to shake. 15 Then a* ***spirit*** *passed before my face;* ***the hair of my flesh stood up.*** (Job 4:12-15)

Do you see the electrical nature of a spirit? "The hair of my flesh stood up." It appears strongly that there is an electrical charge from a spirit. If the energy of vitalism is spirit, then there would be an electrical charge from it.

Not only this, but Luke 10:18 states: *And he said unto them, I beheld Satan* ***as lightning*** *fall from heaven.* Jesus Christ said he *beheld Satan as lightning.* That is pure electricity. Along with this notice: *And no marvel; for Satan himself is transformed into an* ***angel of light.*** (1Cor. 11:14) It is false light, but light nonetheless.

So far then we can see from the word of God that a spirit has an electrical charge, and can also be Satanic, though the reference in Job is not Satanic. Not only so, but what is the energy of your body? Did you ever think about that? What is your energy? Obviously there is spiritual energy and physical energy and I am talking about the energy that keeps you alive. What is it?

According to Taoism Yin Qi and Yang Qi created the universe. In meridian therapy, which we will get into in the next chapter, the Qi flows through the meridians, and those meridians exist in the body and at times touch the skin, which is where the acupoints are.

The word of God states in Romans 7:18: *For I know that in me (that is, in my flesh,)* ***dwelleth no good thing.*** Did you get that? Then the Qi IS NOT A GOOD THING!!! My, My, My, what a little Bible will do to straighten out a bunch of backslidden Christians that are more concerned about their body than they are about pleasing the Lord Jesus Christ. If you are having someone work your Qi then you are being filled with an unholy spirit.

It is this vital force that is the basis for the New Age medicine. Supposedly the vital force can cure any disease you have!

Again though, lets get back to this question, "What is the energy of your body?" To believe it is the vital force is to believe in something no one knows what it is. But the word of God does tell you what the energy of your body is.

Genesis 2:7: *And the LORD God formed man of the dust of the ground, and* ***breathed into his nostrils the breath of life****; and man became a living soul.* Without the breath you would have no life.

Do you know what the definition of Qi is? Qi is a Chinese word and guess what it means in

China. It means BREATH! Now that is a nugget as they say. Why? Because it shows that you are not dealing with mere "electrical energy." It is spiritual energy!

The Chinese claim that when Yin Qi and Yang Qi separate you die. To them it is Qi that keeps you alive. But what does the word of God say? James 2:26a *"For as the body without the spirit is dead."* Then the energy of your body is your spirit! If your spirit departs you die. *And when Jesus had cried with a loud voice, he said, Father, into thy hands I commend my spirit: and having said thus, he gave up the ghost.* (Luke 23:46)

The energy referred to in New Age medicine, or the Eastern medicines is spirit! It is spirit medicine. What the Chinese have not been able to figure out for 5,000 years you can figure out in a few minutes with a King James Bible because the God of the King James 1611 Bible is the Creator of the universe and upholds all things by the word of His power according to Hebrews 1:1-4.

Did you ever think about this? Jesus Christ said:

> John 10:7 *Then said Jesus unto them again, Verily, verily, I say unto you, I am the door of the sheep. 8 All that ever came before me are thieves and robbers: but the sheep did not hear them. 9 I am the door: by me if any man enter in, he shall be saved, and shall go in and out, and find pasture. 10 The thief cometh*

> *not, but for to steal, and to kill, and to destroy: I am come that they might have life, and that they might have it more abundantly. 11 I am the good shepherd: the good shepherd giveth his life for the sheep.*

If you are born again, then you have entered in by the door, which is the Lord Jesus Christ. You have accessed the power of all of creation, which includes the universe. All things are upheld by the word of His power. There is no other way to be saved. All, and He means all, that ever came before him were thieves and robbers. So how do you think the Lord feels when His children start participating in the paths that the thieves and robbers have been trying to use for 6,000 years? It doesn't make Him very happy I'll promise you that!!!

You see, in Eastern religions the medicine is part of their plan of salvation. Therefore the Eastern medicine is religious by nature. They are worshipping what they think is their god, but it is a false god. It is unbiblical medicine. It is spirit medicine. It is satanic medicine that is contrary to the word of God.

God does have a chosen method of cleaning, healing and helping man and his body. It is a method and system that He has chosen from the beginning all the way through to the end. His method is extremely rejected and contrary to all of the New Age medical witchcraft.

There is a system that God has chosen to clean you, heal you and sustain you physically and spiritually in this life and that system is with blood. ***God has always used blood. That is God's chosen method for life, health and purity.***

At the start of the word of God you have Adam and Eve. They have been commanded not to eat of the tree of the knowledge of good and evil. Satan appears to Eve and beguiles her according to 2 Cor. 11:3, and she eats of the tree of the knowledge of good and evil. She thinks that she is doing right but she has been beguiled.

Eve is a very positive lady. She looks for the good in a thing.

> *And when the woman saw that the tree was good for food, and that it was pleasant to the eyes, and a tree to be desired to make one wise, she took of the fruit thereof, and did eat, and gave also unto her husband with her; and he did eat.* (Gen. 3:6)

That it was good for food. That is a good thing. She saw that it was pleasant to look at. That was a good thing. She also says that it was desired to make one wise, and that was a good thing. You see it was the tree of the knowledge of good... and evil. She never looked at the evil, all she saw was the good, and it spiritually killed her and her husband.

She then gives to Adam who knows exactly what he is doing for he chooses to die so he can be with his wife. He gives his life for his wife.

When God returns he calls out, *"Adam where art thou?"* Adam and Eve are in hiding. God judges them and the serpent, and then the first thing he does is shed blood in order to clothe them. God always uses blood for cleansing, whether it is spiritual sickness, or physical sickness. God always uses blood for the cleansing. Let me say that one more time so you will get it, GOD ALWAYS USES BLOOD FOR CLEANSING! *Prov. 20:30 The blueness of a wound cleanseth away evil: so do stripes the inward parts of the belly.* So why would you want to use Arnica? OK, I'm ahead of myself, so let's get back to the subject at hand.

In the next chapter of Genesis, an offering is brought.

> Genesis 4:*3 And in process of time it came to pass, that Cain brought of the fruit of the ground an offering unto the LORD. 4 And Abel, he also brought of the firstlings of his flock and of the fat thereof. And the LORD had respect unto Abel and to his offering: 5 But unto Cain and to his offering he had not respect.*

Cain brings fruit of the ground and Abel sheds blood for his offering. God had respect for Abel's offering, and rejected Cain's. God uses, and chooses, blood for cleansing.

When the law was instituted blood was sprinkled on the book first, and then the people.

> *For when Moses had spoken every precept to all the people according to the law, he took the blood of calves and of goats, with water, and scarlet wool, and hyssop, and sprinkled both* ***the book, and all the people****.* (Heb. 9:19)

The Old Testament could only be in force after death. The New Testament was instituted after the Lamb of God died and shed His blood on the cross. Then the New Testament was instituted. Death had to take place for it to have power. It takes blood to cleanse and bring spiritual health to you and I.

> *In whom we have redemption through his blood, even the forgiveness of sins.* (Col. 1:14)

Along with that the Bible says that the life of the flesh is in the blood.

> *For it is the life of all flesh; the blood of it is for the life thereof: therefore I said unto the children of Israel, Ye shall eat the blood of no manner of flesh: for the life of all flesh*

> *is the blood thereof: whosoever eateth it shall be cut off.* (Lev. 17:14)

I quoted earlier that the blueness of the wound cleanseth away evil. *But he was wounded for our transgressions, he was* ***bruised*** *for our iniquities.* (Isaiah 53:5) In the word of God it is the blood that cleanses, and supports the life of the human body. ***God's chosen method for health, life and cleansing is through blood, whether spiritually, or physically!!!***

You have got to get that! For there is one substance, (when used properly and not offered to him) that Satan can't stand, and one substance that the new-agers avoid like the plague, and it is blood.

I remember hearing a story of a man who had a relative working in a very liberal, modern educated area of Madison, Wisconsin. She was working in a restaurant as a waitress, and fairly new on the job. Being the yuppie place that it was the menu not only had meat dishes, but also listed vegan meals, bean sprouts, tofu, soymilk, and other foods that had nothing to do with an animal of any kind.

The eatery was filled at lunchtime with many people and the young lady was waiting tables. She served a couple of women their lunch and returning to the table not long after serving them; she found that one of the women was distraught. She asked if there was meat or soy in a certain dish. The waitress was not sure but said something to the effect that, I think it is meat, and upon hearing it, the woman instantly puked all over the floor and ran out of the restaurant yelling, "eeewwww, eeewwww!"

It was not a health issue. It was the vegan puking at the thought of eating another animal. That is the mark of a new-ager. They cannot stand meat, or the shedding of an animal's blood so they can eat them.

I like what one preacher said to the waitress when she asked if they were interested in the soy burger. He replied, "Oh No! We only want something that has bled and died for us!" Amen, and amen!

God has said:

> *Every creature of God is good, and nothing to be refused if it be received with thanksgiving. For it is sanctified by the word of God and prayer.* (1 Tim. 4:5)

Yes, the Lord has warned man against the drinking of blood three times in the word of God, and those three times are in the beginning of the word of God, the middle, and at the end, so you are not to drink the blood. But you are to eat the flesh of the animals.

While I'm on the subject, what did God never eat in the Bible? He never ate a vegetable! Yet, in the last days some will depart from the faith... commanding to abstain from meats. What was the first thing God ate in the Bible? When He came to Abraham he ate Beef, bread, and butter!

So scripturally a hamburger is not too far off from being biblical, especially if it is a butter burger like they serve up around Minnesota and Wisconsin.

It does serve to illustrate the point that the Eastern religious spirit that enters you will seek to have you avoid meat. The first meat it will have you avoid is beef! I wonder why? Why would Satan be against you eating beef? In India they worship the cow, and avoid eating it. And India is the heart of Yoga, Buddhism, Ayurveda, and the Kundalini energy of the chakras.

Here are a few things to consider while I am on this subject. When God curses Satan in the Garden He says that Satan is cursed above all cattle. So Satan is classified with cattle in God's classification system. Yet He calls him a serpent, which would put him in the serpentine classification.

Well, take your Bible and turn to Ezekiel 1:

> *6 And every one had **four faces**, and every one had four wings. 7 And their feet were straight feet; and the sole of their feet was like the sole of a **calf's foot**: and they sparkled like the colour of burnished brass. 8 And they had the hands of a man under their wings on their four sides; and they four had their faces and their wings. 9 Their wings were joined one to another; they turned not when they went; they went every one straight forward. 10 As for the likeness of*

> *their faces, they four had the face of a* ***man****, and the face of a* ***lion****, on the right side: and they four had the face of an* ***ox*** *on the left side; they four also had the face of an* ***eagle****.*

Now look at the book of Revelation 4:

> *7 And the first beast was like a* ***lion****, and the second beast like a* ***calf****, and the third beast had a face as a* ***man****, and the fourth beast was like a* ***flying eagle****.*

You can see how they match up. You have these creatures in Heaven around the throne that have four faces. (If there is any doubt about Ezekiel look towards the end of the chapter.) Their bodies are straight and they have feet like the sole of a calf's foot.

Now compare the cherubim of Ezekiel 10:

> *14 And every one had four faces: the first face was the face of a* ***cherub****, and the second face was the face of a* ***man****, and the third the face of a* ***lion****, and the fourth the face of an* ***eagle****.*

Do you see anything different? The faces of the man, lion, and eagle match, but the face of the Ox, or calf is a cherub. And it has a straight body with its soles like calf's feet. You have a cross between a serpent and an Ox.

Now compare this in Ezekiel 28:

> *13 Thou hast been in Eden the garden of God...14 Thou art* ***the anointed cherub that covereth****; and I have set thee so: thou wast upon the holy mountain of God...16 ...I will destroy thee, O covering cherub...*

Lucifer was the anointed cherub that covereth. Right now there are four Cherubs around the throne, but originally there were five. It is rather coincidental because when you study new age medicine they claim that the Ether, or Aura, or Qi, or the quintessence, is the fifth element, and Satan was the fifth Cherub. By the way, five in the word of God is never grace it is always death.

But the face of a cherub is an OX! Or a calf! Holy Cow! Watch out for the sacred cow! Don't have a cow, man! Egypt worshipped the golden calf. The cow is worshipped in India and it is one of, if not the first meat that is avoided by people in the New Age movement. If they keep going deeper they will end up a vegetarian. Why? The New Age movement and its medicine are contrary to God and the word of God. God has always used and chosen blood, and the shedding of blood for health, purity, and cleansing.

New-agers, and Eastern religious medicine avoid blood. The New Age medicine, for the most part, does not operate on its patients, the New Age bibles remove the blood from the readings in many of the places such as Colossians 1:14, and the New Age churches do not like to sing about the blood. God's chosen method is blood, and the New Age method is to avoid blood.

Because of this unbiblical and satanic mindset that permeates the New Age medicine, those who become involved with it end up doing many strange things to their bodies, all for the sake of health and long life.

In Traditional Chinese medicine there is what's called moxibustion. In order to stimulate the Qi/ spirit that they believe is needed for healing they will set cones of incense like substance on certain acupoints of the body, light it and then let it burn out while sitting on your skin. This causes burning, blistering and scars. A cone can be lit and placed on the same place up to five times, leaving permanent scarring. It is no wonder the Christian missionaries of the 1900's termed Traditional Chinese Medicine, *"medical torture."*

There is also what is called cupping. It is where they take a jar and throw a burning peace of alcohol soaked cotton in a jar and then place it over a site on the body and as the cotton burns out it creates a vacuum in the jar that begins to drastically suck the skin of a person causing severe bruising and damage to the body.

Others who become involved in New Age medicine will do colonics (enemas) often, and will even drink their own urine. There is a Hindu medicine that believes cleansing is the key to health. They attempt to clean the toxins out of the body. If you would read your Bible then you would see the key to cleansing is the blood. If you want to cleanse your body then get out and run, exercise and circulate your blood and you will cleanse your body. That is God's method of cleansing. I am amazed at the emphasis on cleansing in many of these Eastern medicines. I think its because they have a sense that they are defiled and dirty. You hear this in the churches as well. Cleanse, cleanse, cleanse! What's the problem? Do you have a sense that you are dirty? If you are saved and practicing Eastern medicine then you may very well be dirty. You are defiled!

But the problem is not physical dirt, the problem with these who practice spirit medicine is that they are spiritually dirty and need to be cleansed by the blood of the Lord Jesus Christ. Again, the remedy is through blood, not through shoving coffee up the wrong way. It is amazing to see what people will do when they get into this spirit medicine that is contrary to the word of God. *But refuse profane and old wives' fables, and exercise thyself rather unto godliness.* (1Tim. 4:7)

I heard of a preacher who peed on a wound he had on his arm in order to facilitate healing. He peed on himself. Folks, that is not natural that is profane!!!

> *2 Tim. 2:16 But shun **profane** and vain babblings: for they will increase unto more ungodliness. 1Tim. 6:20 O Timothy, keep that which is committed to thy trust, **avoiding profane** and vain babblings, and oppositions of*

> ***science falsely so called.*** *21 Which some professing have* ***erred concerning the faith.***

In Yoga they practice what's called Asanas. Those are the various contortions they do with their bodies. They stand on their heads; twist their arms and legs in various shapes. Many of these shapes have animal names like the serpent, or the turtle, dog, or camel. In Yoga these contortions known as Asanas are their prayers to the intelligent energy that flows in their body.

I have a small book, which is entitled "Demon Experiences in Many Lands." It is a compilation of Demon experiences that was compiled by the editor's at Moody Bible Institute. In the book the missionary states that the devils that abided in various people always liked it when the people would harm their selves.

The following is a story about a woman in North China.

> *In the city of Saratsi, North China, we were having a special meetings for women. Coming out of church, we met a woman none of us had ever seen before, who was acting strangely. It did not take long before we knew that she was possessed with evil spirits. We took her into the inquiry room, and sent someone to find out where she had come from and to whom she belonged. Some boys had*

seen her strange actions as she stood outside our gate, and pushed her in. After some searching we found her husband and son, and from them we got the story. They came from a village far on the other side of the mountain range, where we had never been able to go with the Gospel because of the bandits in the mountains.

Her husband told us that she had been possessed for two years. They had tied her with ropes and chains, and had burnt her with hot irons. ***(There is nothing the evil spirits like more than when the person they possess is tortured.)*** *No one in the home had been able to work properly, as she took up all their time. At the last the family talked it over, and decided to take her to the city of Saratsi, where there was a big Devil's temple. There people could go and dedicate their lives to the Devil, and become fortune-teller mediums. But when her family brought her to the city she ran away from them, and it was then that she came to our gate.* (And the story goes on, but I quoted all that for context.) (Demon Experiences in Many Lands, Chicago, Moody Press, 1960, P. 74)

In New Age medicine they do this all for the sake of health by attempting to stimulate the energy, which to them is essential for health and life. What happens though is that they are getting filled with an unholy spirit and defiling their body with spiritual toxins that can only harden and cause them to move further and further away from the word of God.

God's chosen method for life, health, and purification is blood, and that is for the spiritual as well as the physical. To avoid blood is to move away from God's way. The life of the flesh is in the blood. *And washed us from our sins, in His own blood.* (Rev. 1:5)

Chapter

4

ACUPUNCTURE

For thousands of years, darkness had shrouded the land. A land steeped in superstition, fear, and depression. People suffered and searched for light and answers, like so many generations who had gone on before them. One little ray of light had shined 1,400 years earlier by way of the Nestorians, and Satan quickly snuffed it out. But now, many centuries had passed. The end of the Philadelphian period of church history was soon coming to a close, and with it a closing of the open door God had given to the church since 1500 A.D.

The tears, the groans and sighs, of a people suffering from the spiritual darkness of paganism had reached the heart of the true God. The cry of a mother whose child dies from a fever; the Father that stares emotionless after hours of vigil by the side of his bride who has just died of a simple fall; son, daughter, mother and father, people upon people in pain, in sorrow, seeking to survive another day in a land of fear, fighting, and hardship that only seers emotion in order to keep your sanity. This is the land known as China in the 1800's, and these are some of the results of idolatry.

As the Lord looked down and heard the cries of the lost and with a desire for them to come out of their darkness into His marvelous light, he began to speak to hearts of Christians. Christians in England, who had a love for Jesus Christ and a surrender of their wills that motivated them to say as the Apostle Paul did, *"Lord, what wilt thou have me to do?"* I'll go where you want me to go dear Lord.

The Lord Jesus Christ touched, one by one, the hearts of his born again children, to give their life in the service of the King of Kings by going to a dark land known as China. To tell them of the true God who died for them and paid for their sins when He shed his blood on the cross of Calvary. How He was buried and then three days after He arose from the grave victorious over sin, death and Hell. It is a glorious message of light, and He wanted them to go to a dreary land of darkness and let it shine for all them to see.

The method He chose to use would be not only the true specific missionary, but He would use medical missionaries to minister to the physical needs of the people in order to win their attention to the spiritual answer to the blindness that covered the land. Doctors, surgeons, nurses and helpers left the comforts of England, America, and Europe to go preach and minister in the harsh dark land known as China.

The comforts they enjoyed at home were the fruits of people, who loved the true God, worshipped and served Him. It was the fruits of people who honored the correct word of God, prayed and sought His will for there life. God always blesses a land of people whose God is the

Lord. Blessed is that nation whose God is the Lord Jesus Christ. England had Him, but China did not and it showed in the disease, crime, poverty and sorrow that permeated the people.

> *In 1839 there were only two missionary physicians in China; by 1842 more reinforcements had arrived. 50 years later there were 61 hospitals and 44 dispensaries, 100 male and twenty-six female physicians, with a corps of trained native assistants connected to the missionary endeavor. Before the spread of Western methods in China, the Chinese generally had had little knowledge of surgery, but demand for surgical treatment soon far exceeded the capacity of the mission hospitals. In the annual reports of the hospitals in 1895 it was reported that annually no fewer than 500,000 individuals were treated and about 70,000 operations performed, of which about 8,000 were for serious conditions. At first the Chinese had to learn to have confidence in the surgeons, and submit calmly to the severest operations. A patient's relatives were consulted, and usually there were no resentments expressed if a dangerous operation failed.* (Estes, Charles Sumner (1895). "Christian missions in China" (Thesis (PH. D.) - Johns Hopkins University,1895). Baltimore.

OCLC10128918(http://www.worldcat.org/oclc/10128918), http://en.wikipedia.org/wiki/Medical_missions_in_China, 5/15/2010, P. 143)

One of the most famous medical missionaries of the time was a man by the name of Hudson Taylor. With his founding of the China Inland Mission, he labored far inland to reach the lost for the Lord Jesus Christ. He was a medical man and set up medical stations to treat the Chinese who suffered greatly at the hands of their religious medical system. It was the system of Taoism, and the main purpose was to seek immortality, not the health of the individual.

As with other spirit based, religious medical systems blood was avoided. Thus, operations were non-existent up until the western missionaries came in. The demand for true quality medical help was tremendous as evidenced by the preceding article. Through the end of the 1800's and into the early 1900's medical missions labored physically as well as spiritually to help the Chinese people. In almost one hundred years, the pagan, superstitious medical practices of China were virtually eradicated and replaced with the modern western medical system. That is until the Communist take over.

When Communism took over China, religion, and especially Christianity, was outlawed suppressed, and forbidden to be practiced. Along with that take over was the destruction of the medical system, for which it was replaced with the former superstitious system of Traditional Chinese Medicine. This inferior unscientific system was brought back in, and with it came a return of spiritual darkness and suffering.

The following quotes are taken from a text book published by the Peoples Republic of China, Foreign Language Press, 24 Baiwanzhuang Road, Beijing, China 1987. This is an official textbook put out by the Communist Government of China. This textbook is, "*the textbook for these advanced courses*," and "*was compiled by the three training centers.*" This is an official textbook on acupuncture, but I found the following information interesting in regards to the history of Acupuncture, moxibustion, and the Traditional Chinese Medicine.

Written from a communist's perspective:

> *Following the Opium War in 1840, China fell into a semi-feudal and semi-colonial society. The Revolution of 1911 ended the rule of he Qing Dynasty, but the broad masses of Chinese people were in deep distress until the founding of the New China, and acupuncture and moxibustion were also trampled upon.* (Cheng Xinnong (Chief editor), Chinese Acupuncture and Moxibustion, Beijing, China, Foriegn Languages Press, 1987, P. 7)

The narrative will make it look like communism is the answer to everything. The time period that they just covered was the time when China had Christian missionaries walking all over the nation telling the people about Jesus Christ. It is the time when western medicine came in. The reason acupuncture and moxibustion were "trampled upon" was because it is against the word of God and the Christians knew it and could see the suffering that it brought to the people. There is no doubt that it was preached against and warned against.

More from page 7, In reference to Christianity:

> *They denounced and depreciated Chinese traditional medicine and even defamed acupuncture and moxibustion as medical torture and called the acupuncture needle a deadly needle.* (Cheng Xinnong (Chief editor), Chinese Acupuncture and Moxibustion, Beijing, China, Foriegn Languages Press, 1987, P. 7)

Well, look at that! The Christians who were dealing medically with the people preached against acupuncture and moxibustion. That would have been the time of Hudson Taylor, CT Studd, as well as many, many others. The effort to stop the practice was echoed by the government in the early 1900s under Chiang Kai-Shek.

> *Chiang, who was a Christian, wanted to forbid acupuncture by law. Mao knew how strongly the people clung to their ancient method of healing. After he came to power, he introduced it and favored it everywhere.*

(Kurt E. Koch, Occult ABC, Grand Rapids, Michigan, Kregel Publications, 1986, P. 6)

But then communism came in and things drastically changed. So the Christians preached and fought against, the practice of acupuncture and moxibustion and the Communist Party adopted it as their official national medical system.

> *Pg 7, At this period, acupuncture and moxibustion gained its new life in the revolutionary base area led by the Communist Party of China.*
>
> *Pg 8, Since the founding of the People's Republic of China, the Chinese Communist Party has paid great attention to inheriting and developing the legacy of traditional Chinese medicine and pharmacology... It is... simple and economical.* (There is the real reason for its use in China.)
>
> *Pg 10, In the 1950's, China gave assistance to the Soviet Union and other European countries in training acupuncturists.* (Cheng Xinnong (Chief editor), Chinese Acupuncture and Moxibustion, Beijing, China, Foreign Languages Press, 1987, P. 7,8,10)

Yes you can say that Traditional Chinese Medicine, which consists mainly of acupuncture and moxibustion, is the medical system of the communists. It is a system of medicine that was rejected and preached against by the Christian medical missionaries at the turn of the 20th century. These were missionaries who had first hand evidence and knowledge of the effects of this spiritually deadly method of treatment.

Yet in our time, Bible Believing Christians are using this spirit based medicine in an effort to fight disease in their physical body, all the while not realizing that they are being filled with an unclean spirit and defiling their body which is the temple of the Holy Ghost. They are practicing witchcraft, which is a work of the flesh and quenching the Spirit of God at the same time. By the grace of God I am going to show that this medicine is against the word of God and is actually witchcraft.

The Christians referred to the acupuncture needle as the "deadly needle" and in those days they would reuse the needles, which were unsanitary, so I'm sure there was much infection and resulting death. But even today the needles, though sanitary, stimulate an unclean spirit.

I knew a pastor's wife who used acupuncture needles to treat an allergy to wheat. She had needles stuck into her forehead and left them there for many hours. She even came home with the needles in her forehead. She is dead now, as she was taken with cancer and died. The cancer was in her forehead, caused her to go blind, and was extremely painful before she went home to Heaven, for she was saved.

I preached a meeting at a church where there was an older lady there who was a cancer survivor. She and her husband had both become sick. He decided to go natural, and she did not. He died and she is still alive.

I was in another church where I was preaching on the dangers of New Age medicine and there was an older man there. He came to church and had a good kind gentle demeanor. He was a widower who had lost his wife a few years earlier. He later told me that as I preached on the dangers of the New Age medicine that he wondered why I was preaching on a subject like that? As I got farther into the sermon he then remembered how his wife had gone to many alternative medical practitioners for healing, but she had passed away. Her death had shaken him spiritually, and though he had not quit on the Lord Jesus Christ, yet he was not spiritually where he needed to be. Now he began to see the subtlety and deadly effect it had had on his beloved wife. Confusion now turned to understanding and light. With his heart, which for the past few years had been frustrated towards his God, now melted in the realization of the deadly subtlety of this new metaphysical medicine.

While these are just a few stories, and it could be argued that there could be found two opposing stories, with opposite results, yet we will see that Acupuncture is neither godly nor right. It is wrong and against the Spirit of God. It is not hard to show this for the origin of the practice is Eastern mystical religion. If that were all you had to go on, you would have enough to know that you ought to stay away from it.

In the East, such as China and India, the medical systems and the religious systems are one and the same. In the West they are separated so you have medicine, and you have religion, but Shem is more spiritually minded and has recognized that there is a spiritual side to man, as well as to all things. At least, this is how Shem looks at it.

If you don't know who Shem is let me clarify. Noah had three sons, Shem, Ham, and Japheth. Shem is the Oriental, Ham is the Negro, and Japheth is the European. This is found in Genesis 9 and the Bible says that these three men overspread the whole earth. It also says, *"Blessed be the Lord God of Shem."* (Gen. 9:26) Shem is spiritually minded for the most part. He does not look at things the way Japheth or Ham looks at them. When I say spiritually minded that does not mean that He is always thinking about the right spiritual things. Shem is the one that can sit for hours and just use his mind to contemplate things, and usually things in the spirit realm. Semites go up into the mountains, fast and alter their consciousness to enter another world where they think they are getting enlightened. Little do they realize that they are being influenced by Satan himself. This is the origin of acupuncture and moxibustion.

This origin in China starts with what is called Tao, pronounced Dow. It may seem strange that I would start here on a study of Acupuncture, but I think it will help you to know the origin and what is being attempted when they treat you. Acupuncture is first spiritual and then physical. That spiritual aspect starts with Tao.

Tao is their God whom they cannot describe, nor do they even know. When you read their writings and hear their attempts at describing the Tao they end up saying that Tao is beyond description. Tao means "way." Another term they use for their god, and for the condition of their god "in the beginning" is "Wuji," which means undifferentiated unity, beyond vibration. But let me just keep this simple. Tao is their god, though they do not know what it is, for to them, it is beyond knowing. If you could know it, then it is not Tao, or WuWei. The Tao is "nothingness" or the absence of all, or non-vibrational energy of Wu Wei.

What this all means is that they don't have a clue as to what they are talking about. They don't know their god and have no way to find him, or her, or it out. It is a figment of their imagination that, as one deluded fool put it, a "non-definable reality." In other words he was saying, *"I don't know what it is, but I just know it's there."*

The Bible has a description for this in the books of Acts. The apostle Paul was in Athens and while he was there he saw the whole city given to idolatry. This broke his heart knowing that they were deceived and headed for Hell. As he began to preach to the people he said this: *For as I passed by, and beheld your devotions, I found an altar with this inscription, TO THE UNKNOWN GOD. Whom therefore ye ignorantly worship, him declare I unto you.* (Acts 17:23) This is exactly how it is in Taoism. They do not know their god, and are ignorant of not only their own god, but of the true God, the Lord Jesus Christ.

To the Taoists, they believe that Tao is the source of all, but we know from the word of God that Jesus Christ created all things and without Him was not anything made that was made. *He is before all things, and by Him all things consist.* (Col. 1:17)

Bear with me, for I am going to attempt to give you the Chinese mindset, especially when it comes to their medicine. You have Tao, the source of all, yet they do not know the Tao, for Tao is beyond knowing. Then, once upon a time, somewhere far, far away, Tao gave birth to Yin and Yang. Tao, which is non-vibrational energy gave birth to vibrational energy known as Yin Qi and Yang Qi. Never forget that Yin and Yang are forms of Qi. Don't ever forget that! At the heart of acupuncture and moxibustion is Yin and Yang. Like the bulls-eye of a target, Yin and Yang are the center of all in the realm of Traditional Chinese medicine.

Scientific? Not at all! Demonstrable? Somewhat! But that alone does not make it scientific. Yin and Yang are metaphysical, occult, which means it is outside the physical realm. There may be repeatable results, but that in and of itself does not verify the nature of a thing.

So out of Tao, (nothingness), comes Yin Qi and Yang Qi, which biblically are false gods that came out of the Chinese false god called Tao. These are referred to in the word of God as the *"gods of the people which are round about you."* (Deut. 6:14) They are not true gods, but false gods. They are not from the true God, but are satanic in nature, thought and practice. At the heart of all acupuncture are the satanic gods of Yin and Yang.

In Taoism you have Tao, which gives birth to vibrational Yin and Yang, which then do a dance. It can be referred to as the eternal dance. You see Yin is female and Yang is male, and they then give birth to Earth, Wood, Fire, Water, and Metal, also know in Taoism as the five elements. These five elements are also integrated into acupuncture and various medical conditions of health or sickness will line up with these elements. At least in their false deluded medical religious system, that is.

These five elements are then turned into ten thousand things, which we would call this universe. In Taoism Yin and Yang created this universe, so it is not at all a stretch to call Yin and Yang gods, for they are responsible for this creation according to Taoism. This universe is merely an expression of Yin and Yang and is a vibrational energy field that you and I must align with in order to have good health. This is called attunement in some disciplines, but in acupuncture and moxibustion it is merely the balancing of Yin Qi and Yang Qi in your body. You are making the world a better place, according to Taoism, when you balance your Yin and Yang, since all disease, war, and problems come from Yin and Yang being out of balance.

At the heart of Acupuncture is the attempt at balancing your Yin and Yang. All of the procedures have this one goal in mind. Nothing else matters accept the balancing of Yin Qi and Yang Qi. To Taoists that aligns you, in your body, and in your cosmos, or universe. In the Taoist mind set, as with the majority of the New Age medicines, is the belief that you are merely one part of the whole. This universe, this earth, and all things are an integrated whole, of which you are one part. You end up sick or diseased because you are out of balance with the whole and if you can just get back in balance energetically, since it is all energy, then health will be restored to your body and peace will once again fill you, thus bringing joy and purpose to your life.

Doesn't that all sound so good! The problem is that it is all one big lie! You are not to seek to be integrated with this universe according to the word of God. The Bible says; *"Come out from among them and be ye separate."* It also says that; *"Friendship with the world is enmity with God, whosoever will be a friend of the world is the enemy of God."* These religious based medical systems are opposed to the word of God at the root of all that they believe. Their theory for treating disease is Satanic and unscientific. It will grieve the Sprit of God if you get into it, and defile you by filling your body with an unclean spirit.

Just look at the conditions of the countries that practice this type of religion and medicine and you can see that the curse of God is on their land. China is the land of the Dragon. It is the land where the Dragon is worshipped.

Underlying all of the Yin and Yang balancing is the religious aspect of it all and that is to transform yourself into god. The filling, balancing, and working of Yin Qi and Yang Qi in your body is to ultimately make you immortal. The goal of it all is what's known as inner alchemy, which means that at the heart of acupuncture and moxibustion is the attempt at immortality by filling yourself with balanced Qi, and as you submit to the Qi, and become one with the Qi, then you become one with the all and procure for yourself immortality. You see, acupuncture is a form of the Taoists plan of salvation, and if you are a born again Christian you are spiritually fornicating, or cheating on your Saviour when you participate in acupuncture.

Below you have a chart that illustrates what I have just tried to explain. At the top is Tao, or non-vibrational energy. Tao was there before all in timelessness. It is a poor counterfeit of:

> *John 1:1 In the beginning was the Word, and the Word was with God, and the Word was God. 2 The same was in the beginning with God. 3 All things were made by him; and without him was not any thing made that was made. 4 In him was life; and the life was the light of men.*

Tao is at the top, then Yin and Yang, then the universe, then male and female, and then the mess that needs to be reorganized and realigned with the top. This illustrates what Jesus Christ was talking about when He stated, Verily, verily, I say unto you, He that entereth not by the door into the sheepfold, but climbeth up some other way, the same is a thief and a robber. (John 10:1) You see that is exactly what the Taoists are trying to do.

Tao gives birth to Yin and Yang. Yin and Yang give birth to the five elements which become the universe, which proceedes to male and female and ends a mess. Immortality is attempted by reversing the direction as you become one with Qi. *He that climbeth up some other way the same is a thief and a robber.* John 10:1

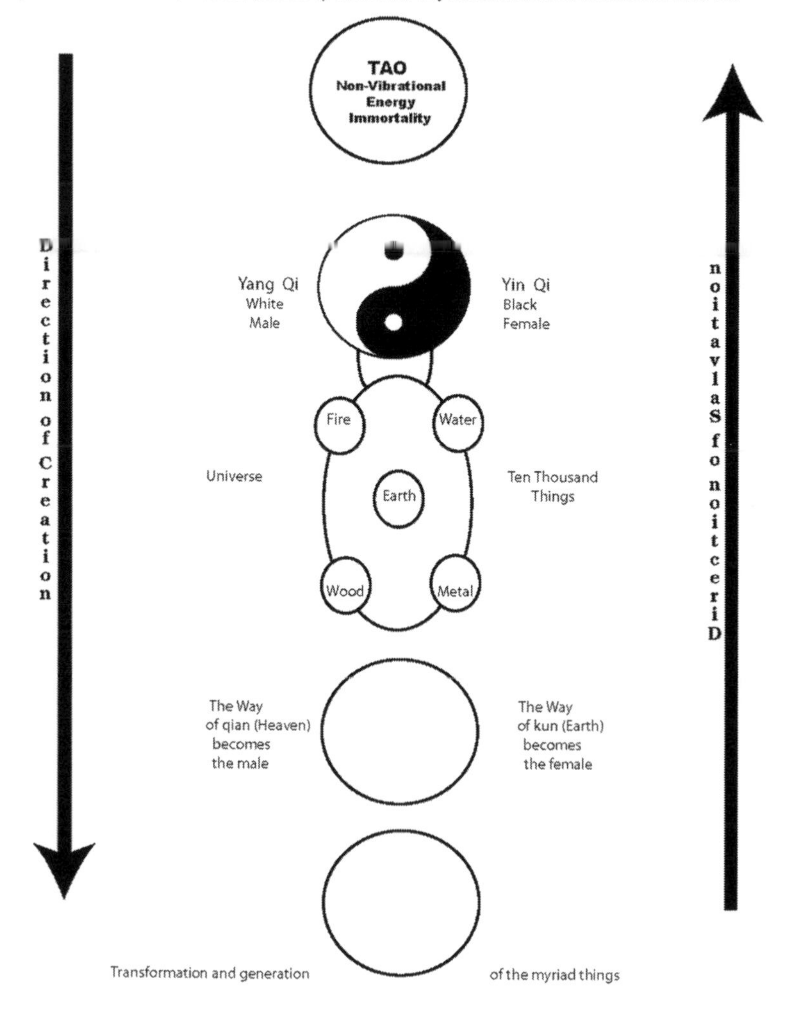

Now you have a philosophical background of acupuncture, which in Eastern Medicine is essential if you are going to understand why it is wrong. Jesus said He that "***climbeth up*** *some other way, the same is a thief and a robber.*" Though you have entered by the door, yet if physically you are using acupuncture you are participating in one of those "*some other*" ways, and practically are no different than a thief. The Saviour is not going to be very happy with you.

But now that you have the philosophy of Acupuncture, lets study the actual theoretical workings of the medicine to see what they are attempting to do and how they go about it. This will be a glimpse into the metaphysical realm of Eastern medicine.

Over 4,600 years ago, if the dating is correct, there lived an emperor in China by the name of Huang-di, or the Yellow Emperor. He is credited with organizing what is known today as Traditional Chinese medicine. The main book that is attributed to him is what is known as the *Yellow Emperor's Classics of Internal medicine* or *Nei-jing*, along with this is also what's known as the *Difficult Classic*, or *Nan-Jing*. These two works are two of the main authoritative reference works on traditional Chinese Medicine. They give detailed accounts of the workings of Acupuncture, as well as an in depth education into Taoism, or the Dao.

I have a copy of this work that has been very excellently translated into English by Dr. Henry Lu, who founded the Traditional Chinese

Medicine College of Vancouver, British Columbia, Canada. This work is what I would term the final authority of Acupuncture, and Traditional Chinese medicine. The information in this book is claimed to be over 4,000 years old, and when they compiled it, the practice of acupuncture had already been around for quite some time for it to be as developed as it is in this book, thus making this information around 5,000 years old. As a matter of fact, modern Acupuncture differs little if any from the acupuncture found in this book.

A few years ago up in the mountains along the border of Austria and Italy a half thawed out body of a man was found. Scientists claim that he is the oldest complete body that they have ever found and date him approximately 5,300 years old. They did an autopsy on him, and found that he had acupuncture points tattooed on his body. The points corresponded to the points he would need to needle in order to treat the medical conditions he suffered from. One was arthritis, and another was whipworm eggs in his intestines that would cause pain in his abdomen. It is interesting to note that the acupoints points tattooed on his body would still be the points today to needle in order to treat the problems that he had. (Editorial Staff, Ice Age Acupuncture?, Acupuncturetoday.com, http://www.acupuncturetoday.com/mpacms/at/article.php?id=27608,8/23/20)

In modern western medicine there is a desire for the latest advancements to be used, because modern techniques are evolving rapidly thus producing superior techniques in medicine each year. But that is not how it is in Traditional Chinese Medicine, for they all look to the Yellow Emperor's Classic as the final authority for their medicine. The textbooks I quote from in this book will be filled with references and quotes from the "Miraculous Pivot" and "Su-Wen." These are books in the Yellow Emperor's Classic of Internal Medicine. It is compiled similarly to the Bible in that it is a book that is made up of books. It is rather interesting to be reading a book that claims to come from over 4,000 years ago. Of course that is nothing new if you have a Bible, for the book of Job will outdate that. But since it is the great authority that all modern Acupuncture doctors look to, then I thought it would be interesting for you to read some quotes from this Taoist medical book.

The scene is the Yellow Emperor asking questions to his medical authority named Qi-bo. In the first conversation of the book the Yellow emperor asks this:

> *I have heard that the people of ancient times lived as long as one hundred and twenty years with no signs of weakening in their movements at that age. But people nowadays become weakened in their movements at the age of less than sixty years old. Is this due to change in natural environments or due to man's faults?* (The Yellow Emperor's Classic

> of Internal Medicine, translated by Dr. Henry Lu, Vancouver, BC, Published by International College of Traditional Chinese Medicine of Vancouver, BC, 2004, Su-Wen, Chapter 1, s1-2)

Well, my, my, my! Here is a Chinese Emperor over 4,600 years ago who was aware that people used to live longer, but now they didn't live as long. If you know your Bible you know that the Lord decreed that man would live no longer than 120 years, at the max, when before the flood they were living over 900 years. And this Emperor wants to know if it is due to Nature, or man's faults. The other word for faults is, Oh my, not that word, it's such a horrible word, oh no the word is...SIN!

But here is an Emperor with this on his mind, asking his medical authority about this subject. His teacher, by the name of Qi-Bo replies:

> *The ancient people knew the proper way to live. They followed the pattern of yin and yang, which is the regular pattern of heaven and earth. They managed to apply the numerical symbols, which are the great principals of human life.* (The Yellow Emperor's Classic of Internal Medicine, translated by Dr. Henry Lu, Vancouver, BC, Published by International College of Traditional Chinese Medicine of Vancouver, BC, 2004, Su-Wen, Chapter 1, s1-3)

So right at the start the Emperor, as well as the reader is introduced to astrologically based religion that is Taoism, which is not surprising for Taoism is at the heart of Acupuncture and Traditional Chinese Medicine. Here are a few more quotes to give you to "amazing wisdom" of this book.

> *Su-Wen 26-3 Qi-Bo replied: Acupuncture treatment dictates that an acupuncturist should await the right moments in the rotation of the sun, moon, and the stars, according to the four seasons and eight solar dates. As soon as the stable state of energy (known as Qi, my comment.) occurs, needle should be inserted.* (The Yellow Emperor's Classic of Internal Medicine, translated by Dr. Henry Lu, Vancouver, BC, Published by International College of Traditional Chinese Medicine of Vancouver, BC, 2004, Su-Wen, Su-Wen, Chapter 26-3)

Doesn't that sound so scientific? You must wait until the planets align, and the Qi stabilizes, and at the right time...SMACK! SINK THE NEEDLE.

> Su-Wen 26-10 When there is the crescent moon, acupuncture treatment should not be administered. (The Yellow Emperor's Classic of Internal Medicine, translated by Dr. Henry Lu, Vancouver, BC, Published by International College of Traditional Chinese Medicine of Vancouver, BC, 2004, Su-Wen, Chapter 26-10)

> Su-Wen 26-37, *Yellow Emperor asked: what is called spirit?*

> *Qi-Bo replied: Let me explain to your Majesty concerning spirit. Spirit refers to arrival of energy (Known today as Qi, my comment) at the spiritual level.* (The Yellow Emperor's Classic of Internal Medicine, translated by Dr. Henry Lu, Vancouver, BC, Published by International College of Traditional Chinese Medicine of Vancouver, BC, 2004, Su-Wen, Chapter 26-37)

That means when they needle they have to wait for the arrival of Qi, or energy, but it is obviously spirit according to their own books.

> Su-Wen 27-18-19, *Qi-Bo: The Acupuncturist should insert the needle to make the energy flow. The acupuncturist should draw out the needle and close the needle hole to prevent spiritual energy, (Qi) from moving outward.* (The Yellow Emperor's Classic of Internal Medicine, translated by Dr. Henry Lu, Vancouver, BC, Published by International College of Traditional Chinese Medicine of Vancouver, BC, 2004, Su-Wen, Chapter 27:18-19)

So when they remove the needle, quick, close the hole so the spirit doesn't escape. If it does then the therapy will not work.

This is from the final authority of Traditional Chinese Medicine. It is superstitious Eastern Mystical practices that have nothing to do with true medical science whatsoever. And then comes the reply; "but it works, but it works, so there must be something to it!"

It may work, somewhat, and I am not saying that there is nothing to it. What I am saying is that it is contrary to the word of God, and as such is satanic at heart. A Christian has no business using acupuncture of any type. At its roots, and really, you don't even have to go to the roots, but at the roots it is nothing more than witchcraft. Psychics are better at Acupuncture than non-psychics.

> *It is a fact of experience that acupuncture is much more successful with psychic doctors and psychic patients than with those who are not psychic. Many Chinese doctors have indirectly acknowledged this, for a great many of them will not treat Western patients by acupuncture. There are of course exceptions, for in the Western world also there are psychic people. Psychic sensitivity, for the most part unconscious, is the catalyst for successful results in acupuncture.* (Kurt E. Koch, Occult ABC, Grand Rapids, Michigan, Kregel Publications, 1986, P. 9)

Here's another "gem," from the main authority of acupuncture, which is one of the fastest growing medical systems in the west.

> Su-Wen s48-33 *Qi-Bo: When the pulse appears like bullets of mud, it is an indication of deficient stomach energy (Qi), and the patient will die when elm-seeds begin to fall in spring or in between autumn and winter.* (The Yellow Emperor's Classic of Internal Medicine, translated by Dr. Henry Lu, Vancouver, BC, Published by International College of Traditional Chinese Medicine of Vancouver, BC, 2004, Su-Wen, Chapter 48-33)

I could go on and on, for I have the book right in front of me. It is full of superstition, Taoism, and Witchcraft. It is no wonder that the Christians fought against it, and Chiang Kai-Shek sought to outlaw it. It is also no wonder that hundreds of thousands of Chinese sought the Christian medical clinics and hospitals for real help. They weren't getting any from the medicine that had been used for the previous 4,000 years.

It is interesting to note that I was recently at a church where there was a single young man who was corresponding with a single young girl who is a missionary in China. He told me that she had been to a local doctor to see if he could help her with a slight medical condition that she had. (She since has stopped after realizing that medicine is against the word of God.) The doctor examined her, and then told her that the westerners are so very different, and that there was nothing he could do for her. He did not know how to treat her...she obviously was not psychic!

Missionaries and Christian researchers who have lived in Asia for many years claim that between 95 and 98 percent of the non-Christian population have psychic powers. These vary considerably in strength, depending on the extent to which the person has been involved with the occult practices of Asiatic religions.

The Western view of life is predominantly based on reason. In the West the percentage of people with psychic powers is the reverse of that found in the Eastern world: between 2 and 5 percent of the population are psychic. Only in those areas where magic is practiced is the proportion a higher one.

What then have psychic powers to do with acupuncture? It is a fact of experience that acupuncture is much more successful with psychic doctors and psychic patients than with those who are not psychic. Many Chinese doctors have indirectly acknowledged this, for a great many of them will not treat Western patients by acupuncture. There are of course exceptions, for in the Western world also thee are psychic people. Psychic sensitivity, for the most part unconscious, is the catalyst for successful results in

> *acupuncture.* (Kurt E. Koch, Occult ABC, Grand Rapids, Michigan, Kregel Publications, 1986, Pg 9)

What was going on was that she was filled with the Holy Spirit, and the Traditional Chinese medicine doctor's unclean spirit medicine did not work. If she continued to go to him though, that all could change, for she would end up taking on an unclean spirit, and once that happened, he would be able to "help" her, for there would be a familiar spirit that could communicate with him. Praise the Lord she stopped before this happened.

In Acupuncture there is the belief in Qi. Qi is the vitalistic life force that is called by many other names in other systems, but it is at the base of the vitalistic belief. Qi is claimed to be "energy." As we have already seen energy, in regards to New Age medicine, is another word for spirit. The circulating and stimulating of Qi in the meridians is what acupuncture is all about. Whether they stick you with needles in your feet or hands, head, or in the eyes, yes they do that; it is all an attempt to stimulate the circulation and flow of Qi.

> *Acupuncture and moxibustion treatment aims at activating the circulation of the qi in meridians, regulating and restoring the normal functions of qi...* (Mao-liang Chiu, Chinese Acupuncture and Moxibustion, Edinburgh, Elsevier Science Limited, Robert Stevenson House, 1993, Pg 42)

As with all metaphysical medicines, the belief that the Qi, Prana, or Ki, is blocked is what they attempt to treat. They are attempting to get the Qi flowing through your body. If Qi is an unclean spirit then you are being filled with an unclean spirit. You are defiling the temple of the Holy Spirit, if you are saved. If you are lost then the spirit of this world will have no problem fellowshipping with the spirit that is being used in acupuncture for they are one and the same. You need to be saved and get the Holy Spirit to enter your body.

The next metaphysical element of Traditional Chinese Medicine that you need to be aware of is what is known as the meridians. The meridians are the channels the Qi that run through your "subtle" body. In acupuncture there is this belief in the subtle energetic body. It is a mystical body of energy that is not physical. It is likened to your astral body, whatever that is. In the word of God you have a body, soul and spirit. It would be easy to give them the benefit of the doubt and say that they were just working with the soul or your spirit, but this would be a grave mistake, for they are working with neither. They are working with spirit, but it is not your spirit for they claim that the "spirit Qi" flows in and out through the acupoints on the skin. That is not your spirit.

Chinese Acupuncture and Moxibustion quoting from The Miraculous Pivot:

> *In the Miraculous Pivot it states that acupoints are 'the joining places*

> *and confluences, 365 in all... and what is meant by the joining places? There are the places where the vital qi inters in and leaves, traveling to and fro,' Later it clarifies by stating 'the joining and converging places, 365 in all, are the sites where the qi of the sub-channels is transported through and pours in.'* (Mao-liang Chiu, Chinese Acupuncture and Moxibustion, Edinburgh, Elsevier Science Limited, Robert Stevenson House, 1993, pg 45)

The qi moves "to and fro," through, and in and out of your body through the acupoints. Hello? Is anybody listening? This is a quote from a book that dates back almost 5,000 years, the Miraculous Pivot.

> *In a very real sense, assuming that it is real (Did you get that? You have to assume it is real.) This energy system may not be considered to be directly a part of the physical body at all, but rather a flow of energy that interacts with a number of energy fields that intersect within and surround the physical body.* (Fred P. Gallo, Energy Psychology, Boca Raton, CRC Press, 1999, P. 34 footnote)

Supposedly then, you have this subtle energetic body. It lies in your body, but is not of your body. It has twelve channels flowing through it. These channels are called meridians, and they run right up your legs, arms, body, and like a lattice, intersect all over your body. They are in your body, but they are not of your body. The twelve main ones have, according to the "experts", definite paths, and the vast majority of books on new age medicine will have charts of the meridians and how they run in your body.

It is interesting to note that most of the meridians end or start either at the bottom of your feet, or on your hands. That is why reflexology works the feet, for they believe that is where most of the meridians start, and by stimulating the Qi even though they may be working your feet, if the specific meridian goes through your lungs, then it can help you breath.

I had just finished preaching on the dangers of New Age medicine and there was a medical doctor in the congregation that evening. Afterwards he was thankful for the sermon as he encountered "Oriental" medicine often in his medical field. He stated that it is becoming more and more integrated into western medicine. He personally was not interested in it, but at the same time acknowledged that it was all around in the health care field, even in the operating room. He then stated, "They don't know why it works. All they know is that it does."

In Donna Eden's book, "Energy Medicine" she tells the following story:

> *I saw an amazing healing while I was teaching a large class in San*

Diego. Within the first half hour, a man in the back of the room had a heart attack and fell to the floor. I couldn't get back to him as a sea of people crowded around. A physician who was sitting nearby did get to him. He began to administer CPR as the paramedics were called. The doctor had clearly become the person in charge, but he couldn't get the man's heart going, and before the paramedics had even arrived I heard him say, "He's gone." My heart jumped into my throat. At that moment, as I anxiously watched the whole scene unfold, a boy of about sixteen suddenly seemed electrified and made his way over to the man. The boy picked up the little fingers of each of the man's hands, put them between his teeth, and chomped down on the sides, at the tips. The man bounced up off the floor, and his heart started beating! Unbeknownst to the boy, those points are precisely at the end of the heart meridian. He said he had no idea what inspired him to do what he did. (Donna Eden, Energy Medicine, New York, New York, Penguin Group, 2008, P. 32)

Yes, he was inspired; there is no doubt about it. When you expire a spirit, your spirit, leaves your body. When you are inspired the opposite happens. Did it work? There is no doubt that it did for the man was alive right in front of them. What a golden opportunity for Satan to deceive a group of people and show them how "superior" Traditional Chinese Medicine is than western medicine.

This reminds me of a story I read in "Say Good-bye to Illness" about the effects of too much energy in a meridian.

> *A 65-year-old man who struggled financially his entire life bought one California lottery ticket. After hearing the winning numbers in the newscast, his granddaughter announced that he had the winning ticket worth 87 million dollars. The man couldn't believe it. He stood up from his chair, took his ticket out of his pocket and matched the numbers that his granddaughter had written down on a paper. When he realized that he had won the lottery, overwhelmed with joy, he fell back into his chair holding on to the wining ticket, staring wide-eyed. Those eyes never closed again. A sudden surge of excess energy flowed into the heart meridian and caused his heart to stop.* (Devi S. Nambudripad, Say Good-Bye To Illness, Buena Park, California, Delta Publishing Company, 2002, pg 48)

You know, that will do it every time. Too much heart meridian Qi, and "Bammo" you're dead!

I wonder how too much life force can kill you when not enough can kill you as well? If disease must have Qi arrive to be cured, why would too much kill you? Well, I'm sure they could explain it.

It would be easy to go into, and explain each and every meridian. So many of the New Age books do this, and it makes them look so in depth and supposedly scientific. But it is not necessary for me to go into each and every meridian. An overview of the meridian system will be sufficient to show its wickedness at heart and unbiblical theory in practice.

In acupuncture there is the belief that running through your "subtle" body are channels, or pathways for the Qi. These pathways are called meridians. In Traditional Chinese Medicine the meridians are one of the essential realities for treatment of sickness, yet, as stated by Elizabeth Reninger:

> These channels exist within the subtle body – you won't find them on the operating table! (Elizabeth Reninger, The Meridian System: Channels of Awareness, About.com, http://taoism.about.com/od/themeridiansystem/a/meridian.htm, 8/23/2010)

This body is also known as your energy body in various circles.

In Chinese theory of medicine, sickness enters your body when Yin Qi and Yang Qi are out of balance.

> *The twelve meridians are the place where life and death are determined, disease is generated, treated and cared for; they are the place where beginners start and acupuncture masters end.* (Mao-liang Chiu, Chinese Acupuncture and Moxibustion, Edinburgh, Elsevier Science Limited, Robert Stevenson House, 1993, P. 31)

There are twelve main meridians, though sometimes it is stated that there are fourteen. The number of main meridians varies, but regardless if twelve or fourteen, there is no way there will be eleven, thirteen, or fifteen. That is because half of the meridians are Yang meridians, and the other half are Yin meridians. Besides the main meridians there are hundreds of lesser meridians. Just think of the streets of a large city and you will have a good idea of what they are like.

1. Lung (arm-yin) and Large Intestine (arm-yang) = Metal Element
2. Stomach (leg-yang) and Spleen (leg-yin) = Earth Element
3. Heart (arm-yin) and Small Intestine (arm-yang) = Fire Element
4. Bladder (leg-yang) and Kidney (leg-yin) = Water Element
5. Pericardium (arm-yin) and Triple-Warmer (arm-yang) = Fire Element (again!)
6. Gallbladder (leg-yang) and Liver (leg-yin) = Wood Element

Elizabeth Reninger, from her article: "The Meridian System: Channels of Awareness":

> *Like a network of rivers nourishing a landscape, the meridians are the channels through which qi flows, to nourish and energize the human body. These channels exist within the subtle body – you won't find them on the operating table! Collectively, they form the matrix within which the physical body functions. They also act as a network of communication between the physical and the more subtle energetic bodies.* (Elizabeth Renniger, The Meridian System: Channels of Awareness, About.com, http://taoism.about.com/od/themeridiansystem/a/meridian.htm, 8/23/2010)

In her book Say Good-Bye to Illness, Dr. Devi Nambudripad states:

> *When the body is in perfect balance, it cannot experience any illness.*
>
> *Chinese medical theory points out that free-flowing Chi through the meridians is necessary to keep the body in perfect balance. In the United States during the 19th century, the founder of Chiropractic medicine, Daniel David Palmer, said, "Too much or too little energy is sickness."* (Devi S. Nambudripad, Say Good-Bye To Illness, Buena

Park, California, Delta Publishing Company, 2002, P. 76)

So six of these meridians / channels, are Yin pathways, and the other six are Yang pathways. Yin and Yang are opposites. Yin is feminine in nature while Yang is masculine in nature. One is cold the other is hot. One is water and the other is fire and so on. While Yin is dark, Yang is light. I mention this for this reason.

In Chinese thought Yin and Yang interact with each other, or against each other. One will overtake the other and vise versa, but this is completely against scripture for the Bible states that, *God is light and in Him is no darkness at all.* (1 John 1:5) There is no mixing of light and darkness, they are opposites and God *"divided the light from the darkness"* (Gen. 1:4).

In the Chinese Satanic belief system, dark and light will mix and interplay with each other thus causing no right and wrong. In Acupuncture, sometimes they strengthen dark, and other times they strengthen light. Dark and light are merely forces (Luke, I am your father. Star Wars!) and either one can be good or bad, it just depends on the situation.

This is completely contrary to the word of God. With the word of God there is an absolute right and wrong. This is not the case in Chinese medicine. The line between right and wrong, good and evil, dark and light is blurred. *Woe unto them that call evil good, and good evil; that put darkness for light, and light for darkness; that put bitter for sweet, and sweet for bitter! (Isaiah 5:20)*

These meridians are said to run right along the body just under the skin. At points along the way they touch the skin and it is these places that are said to be the acupoints, or the spots where the needles are inserted to stimulate the Qi. This is also where the acu-touch is done, as well as the moxibustion. But if the meridians run just under the skin through the body then I know one thing about what is running through the body. That Yin Qi and Yang Qi is *"no good!"*

> Romans *7:18 For I know that in me (that is, in my flesh,) dwelleth no good thing: for to will is present with me; but how to perform that which is good I find not. 19 For the good that I would I do not: but the evil which I would not, that I do. 20 Now if I do that I would not, it is no more I that do it, but sin that dwelleth in me.*

If they claim, and they do, that the Qi runs through the meridians, and those meridians are just under the skin then those meridians and that Qi is no good. It is equated with sin, according to the word of God.

Half of these meridians have Yin Qi in them and the other half have Yang Qi in them. When one of the Qi "energy's" are out of balance then they have to attempt to balance them again. This is done by stimulating the Qi, which is done first of all, by inserting needles into the skin about one forth to one half inch into the flesh. They then may twist and twirl the needles, or they may tap them, flick them, and basically play with them while they are waiting, "for the arrival of Qi." That's right, after they insert the needles they have to wait for the Qi to arrive. Sometimes it is just a matter of moments. Other times it may be an hour, or a day. But when the Qi arrives there may be numbness around the needle, or tingling, or the needle will pull down and feel like a fishing pole.

Imagine that! Here you put a thin needle into someone's arm, leg, or wherever in their body and then you wait for this unknown entity to arrive. Not only that, but in the textbook Acupuncture and Moxibustion it is stated (now keep in mind that these are communists who don't believe in spiritual things) that they must wait for the arrival of the "spirit Qi" and if the "spirit Qi" does not arrive, then the therapy is worthless, and will have no effect on the patient. In the first chapter of *Miraculous Pivot*, it is described that:

> *. . ."acupuncture therapy does not take effect until the arrival of qi". . ."A point is the place where the spirit qi enters and flows out". . . The arrival of qi is a manifestation of the normal activity of the spirit qi.* (Cheng Xinnong (Chief editor), Chinese Acupuncture and Moxibustion, Beijing, China, Foriegn Languages Press, 1987, P. 325)

Even the communists know that they are dealing with a spirit, it's just the dumb Christians that can't figure it out, and I am talking about Bible believing preachers, teachers and their wives.

You are dealing with a spirit; it is an unclean spirit for it runs in your flesh, and if it does not arrive then your acupuncture treatment is worthless. Do you know what you are doing? You are getting filled with an unclean spirit! The word of God commands the Christian to be filled with the Spirit, but that Spirit is the Spirit of God. In acupuncture you are being filed with an unclean spirit.

Sometimes needles are not used. Another form of stimulating the Qi is what's called moxibustion. Moxibustion is where they take moxa, or mugwart herb, crush it, mix it with other herbs, and then form it into a stick that resembles a cigar, or a small cone similar to incense. There are various recipes they use. They then take milk, or something that will make the cone stick, and will put some milk on the place of the body where they want to stimulate. They then stick the moxa cone to the body. (If the cigar shaped stick is used instead of the cone, the doctor holds it over the acupoint after it is lit. It does not touch, but merely warms the acupoint.) It is lit with fire and burns slowly like incense. The cone burns down and is left on the body to burn out on the body. This causes severe pain and blistering. It would be similar to letting a cigar stub burn out while resting on your body. It may be placed up to five times on the same place and left to burn out each time.

It is no wonder that the Christians called acupuncture medical torture. They had seen the scars on the bodies of the people from where the moxibustion was done.

Today, in America, I'm sure this is rarely done, if ever, but as America moves farther away from the word of God, then I am sure that this practice will be performed in a hospital near you in the not too distant future. Most of the modern moxibustion, as I have already described, is done by lighting a moxa stick, which does look similar to a cigar, and burns like one as well. It is then held over the acupoint just off the skin as a form of heat stimulation of the acupoint so as to work the Qi.

There is also the acu-touch, which is where the doctor will just tap or touch lightly on the acupoint in order to stimulate the Qi. This was done to my wife when she was treated for her allergy to dairy products. After the muscle test the Doctor touched Terri on various meridians to balance the Qi, or energy. It was still acupuncture and defiled my wife by letting in an unclean sprit.

Lasers are used as well for stimulation, and electro-acupuncture has been done for many years. Essential oils are also used for meridian stimulation.

Any medical treatment that is working with the meridians is Satanic. Let me say that again. **Any medical treatment that is working the meridian system is Satanic.** Though the Chinese have been very methodical in their observations, and have come up with a very elaborate system of treatment, yet at the root of it all is an unclean spirit and an occult religious system. A Christian should avoid any treatment by such, and if you have been using any form of acupuncture then you need to repent and stop.

All of the Applied Kinesiology systems and their variations are built on the meridian system.

> *Kinesiology and acupuncture have much in common because the development of the former was based on acupuncture theory. Chinese 'I Ching' (Which is also divination.) is the kinesiology of the Oriental medicine, which has been practiced in China for many years.* (Devi S. Nambudripad, Say Good-Bye To Illness, Buena Park, California, Delta Publishing Company, 2002, P. 83)

One last method of stimulation that I have not yet mentioned is that of herbs. The Chinese have been very methodical and have an extensive listing and classification of herbs, herbal remedies, and their uses. Certain herbs are used to stimulate Yin Qi, while others are used to stimulate Yang Qi.

> *Herbs can cause similar healing. Electromagnetic forces of special herbs actually have the ability to*

> *enter selective meridians and push energy blockages out of the body to restore the energy balances. A well-trained herbologist can bring about the same result as an acupuncturist. A combination of acupuncture and herbs can produce excellent results.* (Devi S. Nambudripad, M.D., D.C., L.Ac., Ph.D. (Acu.), Say Good-Bye To Illness, Buena Park, California, Delta Publishing Company, 2002, P. 83)

While I am not totally against herbs, if your herbal treatment has any Chinese basis to it, you need to repent and drop it like a hot rock. While those herbs are natural, that still does not make them safe. Marijuana is natural but it will mess you up - spiritually as well as physically.

> *In Chinese medicine, diseases are often treated with herbs. Applications of Chinese herbs in clinical practice are based upon the nature and capabilities of herbs and they in turn are based upon the energies, flavors, movements and meridian routes of herbs.*
>
> *The four energies of herbs can be broadly divided into yin and yang, with cold and cool energies belonging to yin and hot and warm energies belonging to yang.*

The meridian routes refer to the meridians a given herb is capable of entering and traveling through, which accounts for two herbs with identical energy and flavor still displaying two different actions. In clinical application, herbs are selected that travel through the meridians in the diseased regions.

Although acupuncture and herbology are two different branches of Chinese medicine, with the former treating diseases by external methods and the latter by internal administration of herbs, they are frequently used simultaneously in clinical practice. Both are also based upon the theories of yin and yang, the five elements, the internal organs and the meridians.

The following is quoted in reference to using herbs in Chinese medicine.

...The doctor needs to follow the standard procedures of Chinese diagnosis, which involve the theory of yin and yang as well as the Chinese organ theory. (Henry C. Lu, Chinese Natural Cures, New York, New York, Tess Press, an imprint of Black Dog & Leventhal Publishers, 1994, P. 27-28)

Did you notice that last statement? Yin and Yang are still a theory.

> *For as I passed by, and beheld your devotions, I found an altar with this inscription, TO THE UNKNOWN GOD. Whom therefore ye ignorantly worship, him declare I unto you.*
> (Acts 17:23)

Chapter

5

AYURVEDA

As with China and it's unbiblical satanic system of medicine, so too is India with it's unbiblical and satanic system of medicine. I say that because both are energy, thus, spirit based medical systems that will deceive and mess a person up spiritually. If you are lost and have never been born again then these systems, through the unclean spirit that guides them, will seek to harden you against the gospel of Jesus Christ, as well as keep you deceived into believing the myriad lies that are believed in both medical systems.

> *Jesus Said, Enter ye in at the strait gate: for wide is the gate, and* ***broad is the way****, that leadeth to destruction, and many there be which go in thereat.* (Matt. 7:13)

There are many religions in the world and all of them lead to Hell. I am a Baptist, but being a Baptist will only get me to Hell. There is only one way to Heaven and it is not by religion. But in the realm of religion there are many different types of religion.

If you are a touchy feely type of person then there are religions that are touchy and feely. But maybe you are not like that. Let's say that you are a religious person. You want to worship and do a lot of acts that make you feel good, so there are religions that are that way. You can attend church regularly, and along with your attendance you can stand, sit, kneel, pray, and even study religious subjects.

There are many different kinds of religion and in each of these different types of religion you can become immersed into them. They each can be very deep, in their own way, and intricate in their own way. In each of these religions no doubt there are volumes of books written on the subjects concerning your religion so you can study and obtain great amounts of knowledge.

Along with these great amounts of knowledge you may, or may not, even be helped in your day-to-day life. You may end up with a good marriage, friends, wealth, and any other number of "good" results by becoming active in the religion of your choice. There is one major problem though and that is if it is not the true religion you will end up in Hell, and eventually the Lake of fire.

The many ways, though intricate as they may be, and as temporally beneficial as they may be are all leading you down the broad way to destruction.

So too, it is the same way in the realm of medicine. There are many different disciplines of medicine, and yes, they have results and often times have temporally good results, yet they are against the word of God and the Lord Jesus Christ. Jesus Christ did recommend Doctors for He said, *"They that are whole need not a physician, but they that are sick."* (Matt. 9:12) So if the Creator of the universe, the Lord Jesus Christ recommended physicians then there is a right type of physician, and medicine that a person is to go to for physical treatment of their physical body. Any other medical discipline will be wrong and Satanic in it's origin and operation.

Such are these medical disciplines that I am covering in this book yet, as with religion, so too in medicine, there are many different kinds of medicine from many different places on this earth. In this age that is heading to a one world government that is going to be led by Satan manifest in the flesh, so too then the medical systems of the world are unifying all under the "noble cause" to heal the sick. As Western medicine integrates with Eastern medicine, those who before wanted scientific evidence for the efficacy of a treatment are abandoning that requirement all under the guise of "we don't know how it works, we just know that it does." The results are all that matters now. The adoption of Science falsely so called and the humanistic philosophy of pragmatism are incorporated into the scientific medical community.

Just because you may be helped with a sickness does not mean it is of the Lord. One man told me he never saw anywhere in the word of God where an unclean spirit healed anybody. Yet the Word of God says that Judas was a devil Jn 6:70, and he was given the gift of healing in Matthew 10:1-8. The anti-Christ will have power to give life to an image, and a deadly wound is healed. (Rev. 13) Healing will be one of the false signs used to deceive the world during the tribulation. What we are seeing today is a preliminary of that very thing, and it is in the churches as much as it is in the world. Pastors' wives are playing doctor with homeopathy and muscle testing not realizing that they are practicing witchcraft.

As with Traditional Chinese Medicine, Indian Medicine such as Ayurveda, which incorporates Yoga with its various forms, and the chakras, is full of mysticism, and outright witchcraft.

> *Behind magic, mysticism and also behind the occult the yoga system is present.* (Rammurti S. Mishra, The Textbook of Yoga Psychology, New York: Julian, 1963, As quoted by Kurt E. Koch, Occult ABC, Grand Rapids, MI, Kregel Publications, P. 257)

As the word of God states it is the "gods of the people of the land," (1 Chron. 5:25) and both of these systems seek a unity with the universe and the world that we are living on. Both systems are systematically opposed to the word of God and what the word of God teaches. Ayurveda seeks to emphasize your body and the opening up of your body where as the word of God says to deny your body and mortify it. You are to reckon it dead.

> *Rom. 8:13 For if ye live after the flesh, ye shall die: but if ye through*

> *the Spirit do mortify the deeds of the body, ye shall live. Rom. 6:11 Likewise reckon ye also yourselves to be dead indeed unto sin, but alive unto God through Jesus Christ our Lord.*

When you study Yoga, for example, you see them doing these poses called Asanas, while at the same time mentally passive bodywork outs where their eyes are closed. These workouts, which are the first stage of yoga, open you up to unclean spirits. Kurt Koch puts it this way:

> *The first stage (of Yoga) has the aim of helping the student of yoga to gain control of his consciousness and his body. This goal is achieved by means of mental and physical exercises.*
>
> *The mental exercises include meditation, autogenic training, concentration, and "koan," a litany involving the continuous repetition of a mantra (secret word).*
>
> *The physical exercises include breathing exercises and various bodily postures like the lotus position, the cobra position, and the headstand.*
>
> *This first stage is thus psychosomatic in nature, producing unity of body and mind.*
>
> *There are many Christians who believe that it is possible to participate*

> *in this first stage of yoga without harm. It is merely a matter of relaxation exercises. If only this were true! Counseling experience tells otherwise. This technique of relaxation and these "emptying exercises" so highly spoken of by the yogis lead to the inflowing of another spirit-other spirits. The students of yoga do not notice it.* (Kurt E. Koch, Occult ABC, Grand Rapids, Michigan, Kregel Publications, 1986, P. 257-258)

Chris Lawson, founder of spiritual resource network, tells of Pentecostalism where the people spontaneously start doing Yoga like poses when the "spirit gets moving."

> *Christians undergoing these so-called "awakenings" also* ***assume spontaneous yoga postures and gestures*** *as well as the phenomena noted above. I myself, as a Christian pastor, missionary and researcher, have observed some of this bizarre phenomena in Christian churches when investigating the "anything goes" Toronto / Pensacola / Holy laughter Revival.*
>
> *But these things are no different than the occult phenomena displayed through laughter* ***yoga*** *and* ***Buddhist*** *and* ***Hindu*** *cults. People under this wicked influence imitate* ***animal postures*** *and make*

> *inhumane sounds and movements. They testify of seeing colorful visions, bright lights, and experiencing "t**he Oneness of all things**" (Pantheism). **Practitioners** also hear humming, chirping and buzzing sounds. Even misled Christians have been known to "oink" like pigs, "bark" like dogs, and "roar" like lions. Some, like possessed Haitian Voodoo practitioners, do the chicken dance and are unable to stop until complete exhaustion takes over.*
>
> *Others fall down 'drunk in the spirit' and are physically pinned to the floor by powerful, unseen supernatural powers. It has also been observed in Nigeria that this "**electricity**" type power leads people to "vomit in the spirit".* (Chris Lawson, KUNDALINI ENERGY: Yoga's Power, Influence, and Occult Phenomena in the Church, Spiritual Research Network, http://www.spiritual-research-network.com/yoga.html, 8/24/2010)

These poses in Yoga are called "Asanas", and in Yoga an asana is a prayer. To them the body is the temple and the asana is the prayer. Here is a quote from a very well known Yoga leader, B.K.S. Iyengar "Guruji:"

> *The body is my temple, asanas are my prayers.* (Gita & Mukesh Desai, from DVD-Yoga Unveiled, Gita Desai, 2004, B.K.S. Iyengar "Guruji")

You twist your body into all kinds of configurations and hold them for some time, all the while your mind is to be in quiet passive submission with controlled breathing, and that is your prayer.

Your prayer? Prayer to whom? In the word of God, prayer is asking, but in Yoga, prayer is contorting your body so as to open yourself up to the Prana, which is the energy, and as I have already shown, a spirit. These asanas are all an attempt to circulate, and fill your self with Prana, an unclean spirit, though they do not believe it is an unclean spirit.

There is no doubt though as to the purpose of these asanas. Since Yoga means to unify, there is an attempt to be at one with this energy. The following quote was transcribed from a video of Yoga. B.K.S. Iyengar is Indian, so his English is broken, but this is what he says,

> *So there is a diversity in our body, so when we can bring this diverse body into a single union, then the person whose does himself, having realized the diversity, and bringing of unity in that diversity, naturally it is very easy for him, when he spreads the art of Yoga, how to bring the diverse people to unify, with single thought,* ***of understanding the intelligence that flows in the body, the understanding of Prana, which creates that***

> ***energy, for the intelligence to enlighten more and more.*** (Gita & Mukesh Desai, from DVD-Yoga Unveiled, Gita Desai, 2004, B.K.S. Iyengar "Guruji")

Hello D.D. Palmer and the innate intelligence. Here is a Yoga Guru that states the energy that flows in his body has intelligence, and it is this intelligence that enlightens him. He is dealing with a spirit, and so are you if you are practicing Yoga. You are getting filled with an unclean spirit and you need to repent.

It is so much of the same thing. Whether it is meridians, or chakras, or Kundalini, Reiki, or Pranic healing etc., they are still working with energy/spirit, with the ultimate goal of oneness with the...they don't know...the energy, or "consciousness." In the Bible Acts 17:23 it is referred to as, "*the unknown god.*"

I am so glad I know my God and He knows me. I know who He is, where He is, what He likes, and what He does not like. I know His name, it is the Lord Jesus Christ and He is the Most High God! There is no god greater nor is there any god higher than my God. Not only that, but I am one with Him right now, and He is dwelling inside my body right now.

The attempt at oneness in the Eastern mystical religions, the opening up of their bodies to accept the indwelling of God, and the striving for eternal life are all qualities that I now have in the Lord Jesus Christ. Best of all, all those and more were a free gift when I repented, prayed and asked Jesus Christ to forgive me of my sins, to come into my heart, and to save my soul. I didn't have to twist and shout at all, I just had to believe on the Lord Jesus Christ and get washed in His blood. Ah yes, the blood. Don't forget the blood!

Yoga is a bloodless medical/religious system of works. They claim that the goal of Yoga is to unify the body, for the name Yoga means unity. But along with this desire for unity is the express desire to live and to live well. In the Yoga practice there is an energy that they seek to develop and work. It is an energy system that is centered on what they call chakras.

Have you ever seen the externally serene picture of the young lady, or young man, outside on a hill? The legs are crossed, eyes are closed, peaceful look on their face, and they sit there with the sun shining on them, hands turned up are resting on the knees with the thumb and middle finger together making a circle. The picture conveys a message of tranquility and calmness. They appear so disciplined and in control. Yet, within them is a constant examination that will never let them rest. It is an examination of whether or not they are in balance or out of balance? Have negative thoughts, or has pollution of this modern toxic world knocked their psyche out of balance? The picture appears serene, but on the inside thoughts run in their mind, "Maybe that's why I can't sleep, or maybe that's why I am angry or worried, or maybe, or maybe, oh no I don't know! OK, ...I must calm down, breeeathe, deeeeeply, sloooowwwly, that's right, submit to the energy and balance, think balance and once you get your chakras balanced again everything will be all right."

Now comes the examination of what happened? Did I let my throat chakra get out of balance, or maybe my third eye chakra? So it goes on and on, a relentless self-examination, all for the goal of peace and power thus creating joy and happiness of life. The problem though is that it is all a big lie!

Oh, I am not saying that there are not results. Just as with Traditional Chinese Medicine, yes, there are results, and at times there are good results, at least good to our bodies. But that does not mean it is right! You had better check everything according to the Word of the Creator of this universe or you are going to find yourself in eternal trouble.

I'm sure many experts in the Indian medical system could debate my next statement, but center to the Indian system is the chakras. As the meridians and Qi are central to the Traditional Chinese Medicine, so too Prana and the chakras are central to Indian Medicine.

Prana is the Indian term for energy, though it also means breath, the same as Qi is in China, for it too means breath. As the Chinese work with "energy" known to them as Qi, so too, the Indians work with "energy" known to them as Prana. In both cases it is energy medicine plain and simple.

But, the word of God states that, "*The life of the flesh is in the blood*" (Lev 17:14). God uses blood when dealing with blood filled beings.

Whenever I think of them working with energy I think of Satan attempting to take over Heaven. You see, "energy" is power, and Satan sought the supreme power, and that was to be God. It is the height of rebellion. He said, I will.

> Isaiah 14:*12 How art thou fallen from heaven, O Lucifer, son of the morning! how art thou cut down to the ground, which didst weaken the nations! 13 For thou hast said in thine heart, I will ascend into heaven, I will exalt my throne above the stars of God: I will sit also upon the mount of the congregation, in the sides of the north: 14 I will ascend above the heights of the clouds; I will be like the most High. 15 Yet thou shalt be brought down to hell, to the sides of the pit.*

It was the pursuit of power, ambition and rebellion. Did you notice the, "I will, I will, I will, I will, and I will. Five times he said, "I will". Five in the Bible is the number of death, "*Yet, thou shalt be brought down to the sides of the pit.*"

So too, in energy medicine there is a seeking to be filled with energy, for they think it is the source of their health, peace and happiness. Little do they understand that what they are really doing is being filled with the unclean spirits of devils who are masquerading as results.

The following story I am going to use to introduce you into what I am talking about, though in this story the results are not specifically a "healing," yet it illustrates how they are working with unclean spirits. The story is from Energy Medicine, by Donna Eden, and has to do with a woman's "Root Chakra":

> *I recall, for instance, touching into the energy of a woman's root chakra and strongly sensing that I was going to find disease in her body. To my surprise, as I explored the energy of each of her chakras, looking for the one that carried the illness, she appeared to be very healthy. Returning to her root chakra, and going deeper and deeper through its layers, however, I became absorbed in a terrifying sense that death was imminent. While I could find no diseased energy, this terror about dying was embedded in every layer of her root chakra.*
>
> *I began tuning in to painful stories rising up from what felt like previous generations, mostly concerning the women of her family: dying during childbirth, starving on the prairie, characteristic deaths for the times. A feeling spiraled up from her root chakra that seemed to say, "No one can save me; nothing can be done; I'm not going to survive!" I related*

this and explained my sense that the feeling that she wasn't going to survive belonged, I believed, to her ancestors, not to her.

"All my life," she said, "I've believed death lurked around the next comer. I have never understood it. I've been in therapy trying to find out if some childhood trauma had caused my death fears. I've often run to doctors, just to make sure I'm really well. I can't even commit to a relationship because it seems unfair when I know I might die at any moment. I know it makes no sense, but it is an overwhelming force that comes up in me, and this feels like the key I've been looking for." (Donna Eden, Energy Medicine, New York, New York, Penguin Group, 2008, P. 160-161)

What you have here is a woman who is practicing spirit medicine, and I am sure she means well, but "her experiences" would appear to parallel that of a fortuneteller, and of one that has a familiar spirit. There is no doubt that what she discovered here was by supernatural means. As such it is a form of divination for it is revealing hidden knowledge through supernatural means.

I included this story to introduce you to the chakras. The so-called spinning discs of energy that line your spine all the way up to the top of your head.

Central to Indian medicine are the chakras. What are they? Are they even real? Well, you won't find them on the operating table either, just like the meridians of Traditional Chinese Medicine (TCM). The whole Indian medicine system is built around these chakras. Yet it is uncertain how many there really are. As with TCM and the meridians which some people say there are 12 main meridians, and others say there are 14 main meridians, so too, in Ayurveda it varies as to how many chakras there really are. It is generally accepted that there are seven major charkas.

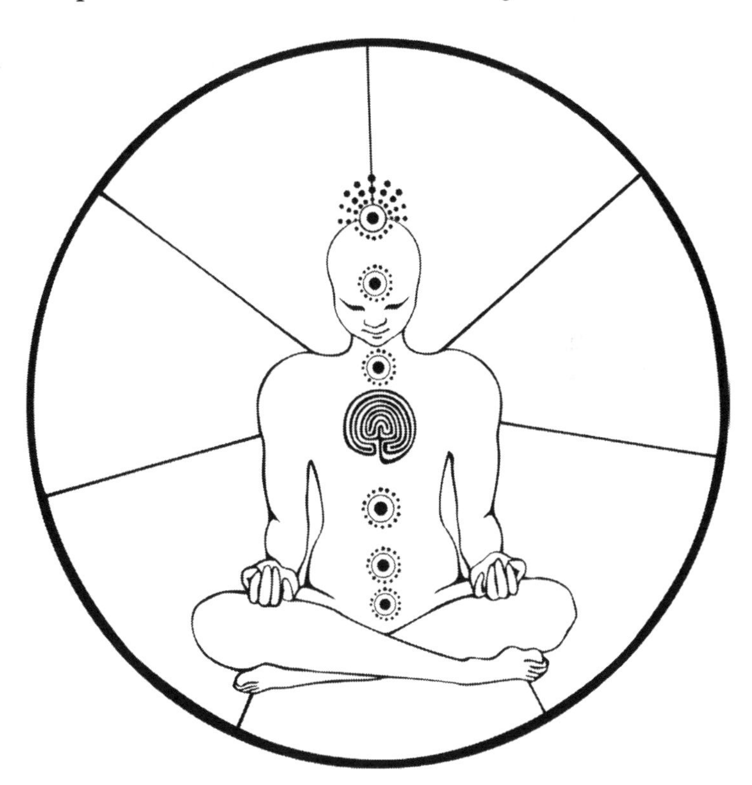

Donna Eden states:

> *Seven major chakras are usually distinguished, although I've heard of systems that identify only five major chakras and others that set the number as high as ten. Part of this discrepancy may be because there are also many minichakras throughout the body. The hands and eyes act as chakras, and new spiraling vortexes may appear anywhere that fresh energy is required, such as after an injury or if an area needs to be cleared of toxic energies.* (Donna Eden, Energy Medicine, New York, New York, Penguin Group, 2008, P. 153)

Why the discrepancy? Well, one reason is that you are not dealing with the physical. In real medicine it is obvious what the organs are and how many of each there are. A person has two kidneys or one liver and that is true of normal people all over the world. But when you get into the metaphysical realm there are no absolutes so it is all in generalities. As it says in Acts 19:19, they are *"curious arts."* They are curious because you are never really certain of anything about them. Because of this they then point to the results and proclaim, "See it works!"

Well, these chakras are said to be spinning vortexes of energy. Kind of like a spinning daisy wheel. They are said to be located up your spine, inside your body. According to Dr. Deepak

Chopra then they are vortexes of Prana, which would make them identical to the Qi of Traditional Chinese Medicine, and here we go again. What you are dealing with is "spirit" manifestations, not merely benign vortexes of energy, though this is what thy try to make you think.

Keep in mind that the energy of this medicine is metaphysical in nature and therefore there will be no way to come to absolutes. It will fall under the realm of those "curious arts" in Acts 19:19.

Donna Eden:

> *The chakras are spirals of energy that are a focus in the practice of yoga and are addressed in a variety of healing systems. These energy fields apparently spiral above and, at the same time, permeate specific areas of the body, and they also interact with the energies that surround the body. Pioneering research in the 1970s by Valerie Hunt at UCLA's Energy Fields Laboratory demonstrated that specific regions of the skin produced very rapid electrical oscillations (up to 1,600 cycles per second, as contrasted with 0 to 100 cycles per second in the brain, 225 in the muscles, and 250 in the heart3) with ancient descriptions of the body's "chakras." Spectrogram analysis4 and a special type of photography5 also revealed distinct frequency ranges or colors associated*

> *with specific chakras.* (Donna Eden, Energy Medicine, New York, New York, Penguin Group, 2008, P. 152-153)

Again they pull out the machine to measure the electrical charge that is associated with each area the chakra is known to reside in the body, but this only shows the presence of a spirit for in the book of Job when a spirit passes before Job the hair of his flesh stands straight up showing the very strong likelihood that spirit has an electrical charge to it. I know that the energy of my body is my spirit and they have proven it is an electrical charge that moves through your body. Since the energy of your body is your spirit then a spirit has an electrical charge associated with it.

At the risk of being redundant, I am going to state it again; God has chosen blood for His divine method of life, health, and cleansing for you spiritually and physically. You had better be concerned with your blood instead of energy. Not only is this biblical, but also when it is all said and done, those who work with energy don't know exactly what the energy is, and they never will in this life, unless they accept the truth the Word of God on this subject.

When these new age machines are measuring the electrical charges of things they are measuring the spirit of the thing, or in their terms the Qi, Prana or Aura, or Ether. There are many names for the same thing. Yes, it is energy, but it is not solely electricity, for in Yoga the Prana has its own intelligence, just as it does in muscle testing, Reiki, and other spirit medicines.

When Donna Eden mentions that there are *"also many minichakras throughout the body"*, this would easily fit with scripture, but not in a positive way. In the gospel of Mark there is a man mentioned in chapter five that has an unclean spirit. The story is mentioned also in the book of Matthew in chapter eight, yet two men are mentioned in Matthew, but in Mark he singles one out for the story. Jesus Christ casts the unclean spirit out of the man that consisted of 1,000 unclean spirits. This would be 1,000 for each of the men. Now that would be a body with many chakras in it for sure.

According to Indian medicine there are seven main chakras. These spinning discs of energy are located right up the center of the body. The root chakra is at the base of the spine and then there are six more with the sixth being the third eye, right between the eyes, and the seventh being on the top of the head which is known as the crown chakra.

The chakras are widely used in witchcraft. You will find them in books on witchcraft more often than the meridians of acupuncture are found in books on witchcraft. It is also very common to find them on witchcraft web sites.

Quoted from The Complete Idiot's Guide to Wicca and Witchcraft:

> *Because the quality of your energy can affect your magick, you want your energy to be as clear and strong as it can be. And your attitude toward*

> *your goal, your magick, and yourself will also affect your energy and the outcome of your magick.*
>
> *CHANNELING CHAKRAS*
>
> *The seven chakras are energy centers in the body that lie along your spine. Each chakra picks up and sends out a specific type of energy. Imagine them as wheels of spinning energy.*

After going through the other six chakras you then read this:

> *The seventh chakra, the crown chakra is at the top of the head. This last chakra is our spiritual door, our connection to spiritual wisdom and the All.*
>
> *If you have energy blockages in any of your chakras, they will negatively affect your magick by making it difficult for you to send or receive certain types of energy. You can work to open your chakras by meditating on the area of the chakra in your body... A blockage in a chakra usually has physical manifestations.* (Denise Zimmermann, Katherine Gleason, Miria Liguana, The Complete Idiot's guide to Wicca and Witchcraft, New York, New York, The Penguin Group, 2006, P. 217)

Quotes from the Encyclopedia of Wicca and Witchcraft:

After going over the Eight-Fold Path for magickal and religious training that they say *"must be mastered in order to become an adept or master of the Craft,"* they then write the following:

> *These eight traditional aspects of magickal/religious training within Wicca/Witchcraft can be found in shamanistic traditions throughout the world as well as in the mystical disciplines of Eastern practices. Tantric yoga is a good example of the Eastern practice wherein the kundalini force is evoked. The eight-fold path is a guideline to those who are interested in what the ancients believed to be the necessary steps to personal power. A personal study of each of these aspects will provide the Wiccan/Witch with the tools through which deeper levels of magickal knowledge can be obtained.* (Raven Grimassi, The Encyclopedia of Wicca and Witchcraft, St. Paul, Minnesota, Llewellyn Publications, 2003, P. 138)

So according to the Encyclopedia of Wicca and Witchcraft, the practice of the Eastern disciplines, such as Yoga will enable you to have more power for witchcraft. The two fit together like they were made for each other.

You may wonder why I am putting all these quotes in here? The reason is to show that Yoga, the chakras, and Indian energy medicine is witchcraft. Did you know that witchcraft is a work of the flesh that a Christian can get caught up in? (Galatians 5:19-20)

The "Root Chakra" as it is called, is at the base of the spine and they say its color is red. It is interesting to note that the adrenals are associated with this chakra. It is very common for one who goes to a New Age doctor, and especially if they are a woman, to be diagnosed with "Adrenal fatigue". It sounds like someone is messing around with the chakras, which is actually a form of witchcraft.

The root chakra is said to be the "I am" chakra. Isn't that interesting? The name the LORD uses when Moses asks:

> Ex. 3:13 *And Moses said unto God, Behold, when I come unto the children of Israel, and shall say unto them, The God of your fathers hath sent me unto you; and they shall say to me, What is his name? what shall I say unto them? Ex. 3:14 And God said unto Moses, I AM THAT I AM: and he said, Thus shalt thou say unto the children of Israel, I AM hath sent me unto you.*

So in Indian Medicine "I am" is at the bottom of the spine. Yet the highest chakra, which is associated with Kundalini, the serpent, is at the top of the head. If you cannot see that is satanic you are willfully blind.

Along these lines, notice this next quote from The Encyclopedia of Wicca and Witchcraft:

> *The incarnation of these images is one of the goals of ______ Magick. Another goal is to raise a form of power from the base of the spine. In this area resides the kundalini or serpent power that has been suppressed for centuries by the Christian church. The goal is to bring this energy up to the third eye, where it will give the person almost unlimited power.* (Raven Grimassi, The Encyclopedia of Wicca and Witchcraft, St. Paul, Minnesota, Llewellyn Publications, 2003, P. 366)

The third eye is the sixth chakra located right between your eyes in the center of your forehead. The place where Roman Catholics put the ashes and married Indian women put the red dot, and the place where the Anti-Christ will put his mark 666.

Well isn't that interesting! Here is an encyclopedia on Wicca and Witchcraft and it is telling how to work your chakras so as to raise the serpent power in your body to give you almost unlimited power. That is the exact goal of Yoga. When they begin to do the asanas; those physical contortions of the body, they are working the serpent power, also known as Kundalini, just like the witches do.

Here is another description of the integration of witchcraft and the chakras. The portion you are about to read is from the description of Baphomet, also known as Satan incarnate in some circles. Again, this is quoted from The Encyclopedia of Wicca and Witchcraft:

> *Baphomet's belly is covered with scales symbolizing Water, which itself represents the emotions. The belly is a chakra point linked to the spleen and the endocrine system. Thus the scales symbolize purification and health through balancing...by the serpents encircling the rod of the caduceus.*
>
> *Enclosing the chakra area is a circle representing the dome of the heavens...* (Raven Grimassi, The Encyclopedia of Wicca and Witchcraft, St. Paul, Minnesota, Llewellyn Publications, 2003, P. 41)

Is there any doubt as to the nature of Yoga? This would fit right in line with Yoga, for in the four steps of Yoga; the last degree is where a person is immersed into the darkest of all witchcraft.

Kurt Koch quotes from a book by Rammurti S. Mishra on Patanjali Yoga. The name of the book is The Textbook of Yoga Psychology and is considered the definitive work on Yoga and is used as a textbook. Keep in mind that the chakra system is at the heart of Yoga. He states:

> *A. The higher ego of man is transcendent and immanent, without*

> *beginning and without end, it has no birth and no death.*
>
> *B. Yoga means the synthesis of the physical and metaphysical universe.*
>
> *C. Heaven and Hell are only products of the human mind.*
>
> *D. Behind magic, mysticism and also behind the occult the yoga system is present.* (Rammurti S. Mishra, The Textbook of Yoga Psychology, quoted in Kurt E. Koch, Occult ABC, Grand Rapids, Michigan, Kregel Publications, 1986, P. 257)

There are four stages of Yoga. The first stage is to gain control of your body and mind. Many Christians think they can participate in this level and they will be safe, but it is only a doorway that leads them to having fellowship with devils.

The word of God states that you are not to fellowship with the unfruitful works of darkness. You are to separate from them. Putting a smile on the face of Jesus Christ ought to be more important than your own personal health. That may be a hard statement if you are in pain, but it is still the truth.

> 2 Cor. 6:14 *Be ye not unequally yoked together with unbelievers: for what fellowship hath righteousness with unrighteousness? and what communion hath light with darkness? 15 And what concord hath Christ with Belial? or what part hath he that believeth with an infidel? 16 And*

> *what agreement hath the temple of God with idols? for ye are the temple of the living God; as God hath said, I will dwell in them, and walk in them; and I will be their God, and they shall be my people. 17 Wherefore come out from among them, and be ye separate, saith the Lord, and touch not the unclean thing; and I will receive you, 18 And will be a Father unto you, and ye shall be my sons and daughters, saith the Lord Almighty.*

The Second stage of yoga involves the control of the unconscious mind. At this stage you can control your visceral nerves and make wounds appear on various places of your body just by thinking.

The third stage of yoga is concerned with the mastery of the natural powers. At this stage the student is able to heat objects by mental concentration. This may sound far-fetched but I was with a pastor who before he was saved had been into Kung Fu. Being fairly new at it though, one day the group he studied with was headed to a Kung Fu competition. As they sat in the van on the way he noticed one of the other students had taken a metal rod and wrapped it in a wet paper towel. As they traveled to the meet he sat and stared at the metal rod wrapped in the wet paper towel as he was holding it in his hand, and after some time steam started to rise from the paper towel.

This pastor, who again was lost at the time, asked one of the other young men, "What is he doing?" They said that he was focusing his Qi.

> Koch continues: *At the forth stage, the yogi gains the mastery of the dark arts. The Lamas of Tibet are particularly well known for this. I have collected very many examples of stage four yoga. In Kalimpong on the Tibetan border, I came into contact with many Tibetans. I have also received reports from former missionaries in Tibet. Especially enlightening was the confession of a man who has given me permission to publish his story.*
>
> *Ex 273 My informant had studied yoga, magic and spiritism for ten years with the Lamas...He said, 'what the Lamas teach is the cult of spirits, the cult of demons. Please help me to become free.' We had a long talk together. From this man I learned that the tibetan yogis are masters of the trance, materialization, excursion of the soul, telekinesis, levitation, perfectly controlled telepathy, and all the arts of spiritism. At stage four, which I have met in this intensity only with Tibetans, Zombis, Alauts, Maccumbas, and voodooists, yoga can no longer, with the best will in*

> *the world, disguise its true character. Here yoga reaches its ultimate master - Satan, whose desire it is with his promises and his wiles to snatch people away into the abyss.*
>
> *There is no need for further comment on the religious side of yoga. Yoga ends not only in self-redemption and atheism, but in the cult of demons. Those who undertake to take part in yoga exercises enter a force field by which they are unwittingly directed towards the origin of these powers. These are the powers of which Paul speaks in his epistles, (see Colossians 2:15). Christ has freed us from the spirits, demons, and powers. The chief of these powers is Lucifer, who is seeking to win back those he has lost. And what success he has gained, for yoga has become the fashion in the West!* (Kurt E. Koch, Occult ABC, Grand Rapids, Michigan, Kregel Publications, 1986, P. 258-260)

To be thorough, I must write somewhat of what's known as Kundalini. I have written some already, for at the foundation of Yoga, is Kundalini.

Located at the base of the spine, (again this is according to Indian medicine) is a Pranic form of energy known as Kundalini and it is described as a serpent coiled up three and one half times. (It is amazing how specific they can be about something they are not sure of what it really is.) It lies dormant until the person seeks to awaken Kundalini. In some of the information that I have read, even in witchcraft books, they warn against the awakening of Kundalini, for they say that it is a very powerful energy and if you are not mature enough the energy can harm you.

This seems strange, for in Yoga the purpose of Yoga is to develop and work with Kundalini. The practice is to work Kundalini up through each chakra and then back down to your root chakra. In Yoga you will see them doing exercises that make them look like a serpent moving. This is to awaken Kundalini. Of course Jesus Christ stated: *Ye are of your father the devil, and the lusts of your father ye will do.* (John 8:44) To exercise and act like a snake slithering is not what I call healthy. They then have you pant and stick out your tongue at times.

> *It is important to note here that demonic power [kundalini energy] is the basis of all occult belief systems. It is called by many different names around the world but in the end it is always viewed as an impersonal "force", "energy" or "power". Kundalini energy, the foundation and core of Hinduism's pantheistic (and pan-en-theistic) belief system, is the exact same power that fuels idolatry and the open worship of demons in countless other religions,*

> *not just Hinduism. Furthermore, the awakening of kundalini energy, also known as kundalini arousal, is the ultimate aim of all yoga practice. Interestingly, most Western yoga instructors never mention this and many of them will purposefully avoid talking about it.* (Chris Lawson, "KUNDALINI ENERGY: Yoga's Power, Influence, and Occult Phenomena in the Church", Spiritual Research network, http://www.spiritual research network.com/kundaliniyogaoccultchurch.html), 8/224/2010)

Does this sound like something you would want to cultivate? If you are a Christian who loves your Lord and Saviour Jesus Christ you will have no part in this sort of thing, yet there are those who will say that they are not doing that. They are merely doing the Yoga for the exercise of it all. Can't you find something else? Surely there is some other way to exercise your flesh without taking part in Satanic Pagan practices. More and more Christians are getting caught up in this wicked activity all for the sake of better physical health, yet all the while they are grieving the Holy Spirit that dwells inside their body.

Whether you practice Yoga and chakra balancing out of ignorance, or out of rebellion by purposefully ignoring it's true origin, then you are opening yourself up for real problems. You cannot dabble in sin and get away with it. You cannot play games with your Saviour and get away with it. So many people are deceived into thinking that now that they are saved and don't have to worry about going to Hell, then they can live like they want to with no consequences, and nothing could be farther from the truth.

If you are saved then you have been bought with the blood of the Lord Jesus Christ; He owns you! For you to ignore Him, or nominally acknowledge Him in your life is not only sin, but an attitude of selfishness that is described in 2 Tim 3:2, *"Lovers of their own selves."* It is an attitude of the Laodicean age that we are in and plays right into the hands of the devil. The Bible says that, *the backslider in heart shall be filled with his own ways, (Prov. 14:14)* and that is what will happen to you if you keep loving yourself more than you love the One who died for you on the old rugged cross.

All of these Eastern religious medical systems are completely opposed to the word of God. By that I mean that they are opposite of what the word of God teaches. In this modern mindset people think that God is being selfish for demanding that you love Him supremely, and that you are to have no other gods before Him. The wicked satanic depraved nature of man that has been manipulated by the god of this world strikes out in rebellion and shakes his fist in the face of God so as to say, "Whom do you think you are to demand that I serve you? What about what I want to do? I'm not as bad as my neighbor, and after all you made my body, so I must take care of it."

So you get into Yoga, Qigong, Reiki, or any of the other myriad touchy feely health conscious activities and the result is that your thoughts, actions, and heart are all turned towards yourself. All of these activities go against the word of God in that they turn your focus on yourself. Self, self, self, that's what becomes the center of your universe, when the word of God commands for you to deny yourself, mortify yourself, and to reckon yourself to be dead indeed unto sin and alive unto Jesus Christ.

I mention Reiki here for a reason. Reiki is a form of Japanese spirit medicine that compared to Traditional Chinese Medicine, and Ayurveda, is a new kid on the block, though its roots go back to Buddhism. It has not been around all that long, but Reiki is increasing dramatically in popularity, and is being used more and more in hospitals in America, as elsewhere in the world. According to a June 22, 2009 article in Reiki News, 15 percent of the hospitals in the United States are using Reiki.

The reason that I mention it here is because, not only is it a very popular spirit medicine being practiced in America, but also because of its origin, and how it started. A man started Reiki by the name of Mikao Usui, and he was born on August 15, 1865 in the village of Yago in the Yamagata district of Gifu prefecture Japan. He was a very educated man, but later in his life his business was failing, and being the sensitive spiritualist that he was, he decided to go up into the mountains and meditate in various "power spots," just like they claim to have in Sedona, AZ. While up in Mt. Kurama he had enrolled in Isyu Guo, a twenty-one day training course which likely consisted of meditation, fasting, chanting and prayers.

It is believed by some Japanese Reiki masters that Usui Sensei one day went to a power spot, which is located under a waterfall on Mt. Kurama. Still today, people go there to meditate. The practice is to stand under the waterfall and let the water flow over the top on your head. As one meditates there the striking of the water on the top of the head, and the flowing of the water over the head activates the crown chakra.

Oh, here we go with Kundalini again and the chakra system. Usui is using the satanic chakra system.

Anyway, Usui, while up in the mountain meditating had his crown chakra opened and the Reiki energy entered his body thus greatly enabling his healing powers. After this "enlightenment" Usui started his own school to teach the art of Reiki. That is the start of Reiki and it was in the early 1900's. Yet, its root is in the chakra system.

Reiki is considered a form of healing touch and there can be no doubt that it is an energy/ spirit medicine. Yes, healing touch is an energy spirit based system that is contrary to the word of God. Many nurses are using healing touch in the hospitals.

I had one administrator attend a revival meeting where I preached on New Age medicine. After the service she said that that very day she and the other workers had been instructed by a very famous clinic to start touching the patients more for there is healing in your touch. If it is simply touching, well maybe that would be Ok, but this was more than mere touching. It was the transference of energy that was the goal.

Here is an example of a Reiki session from: The science of the craft: modern realities in the ancient art of witchcraft:

> Gentle music plays in the background. A trickle of smoke, the fresh sharpness of cedar incense, rises in the air. In the back room of a New Age bookstore, a Reiki master focuses her thoughts. *"Lords of Reiki, let the Reiki energies flow..."*
>
> She visualizes a symbol, passed down to her from the Reiki master who gave her her attunements, and feels her hands growing warm. Before her, lying on a folding massage table, her client waits with closed eyes ad shallow breaths... a bit nervous, perhaps, about this foray into alternative medicine, a literal laying-on-of-hands.
>
> The client is a carpenter in his late fifties, a successful man with a reasonably prosperous business... but lately the first pangs of arthritis have been gnawing at the fingers of his hands and making it hard, some days to work his tools. He's been going to his doctor, but all she's been able to offer is aspirin and other pain

relievers that might ease the pain for a few hours but don't really help the stiffness.

His wife was he one who urged him to come here today. She'd come to this Reiki practitioner for her sciatica and claimed the sessions helped her a lot. The whole thing still feels a bit foolish, but he's agreed to give it a try.

The master touches the man's scalp, her hands slipping into the first position, cradling his head. Her hands feel very hot, now, and as she continues to focus her thoughts, she can feel the familiar tingle of Reiki energy flowing through her body, through her arms and hands, and into the man before her.

Unlike some other forms of energy work, the energy comes not from within the healer, but from the universe around her. Ancient Asian teaching holds that we live and work and breathe within a sea of energy, and that those who know how can tap this sea, allowing their bodies to become conduits for healing life force. What the ancient Hindus called *prana* and the Chinese called *chi,* the Japanese call *ki,* the "ki" part of the word Reiki, which means, roughly, "divine energy" or "universal life energy."

> She feels the ki flowing....
>
> And her client, in the midst of a thought to the effect that this is sheer nonsense, stops. The woman's hands are hot, as though She'd held them under running hot water for several minutes, and he feels... *something.* A kind of a tingle spreading out from the points where her hands are touching him.
>
> He feels... relaxed. With the soft music going, it would be so easy to drift off to sleep. Odd. The pain in his hands is a bit less. Experimentally, he flexes one hand. Sure, the pain's still there... but muffled, distant somehow, and it seems to be fading, moment by moment. The stiffness is easing too.
>
> *_______, that's weird!... (Word omitted, due to discretion)* (William H. Keith, The science of the craft: modern realities in the ancient art of witchcraft, New York, New York, Kensington Publishing Corp., 2005, Pg 136-137)

Yes, it is weird because you are being filled with an unclean spirit.

The spirit energy of Reiki is said to have its own intelligence. There are many different terms for this intelligence in the Reiki energy but one that seemed so strange to me was that it was called the Zoom energy. This Zoom energy knows where it needs to go and what it needs to do so as long as the Reiki master can "hook up" to you then it doesn't matter what part of your body they touch, the energy knows where to go and what it must do.

> *Reiki can be defined as a non-physical healing energy made up of life force energy that is guided by the Higher Intelligence, or spiritually guided life force energy. This is a functional definition as it closely parallels the experience of those who practice Reiki in that Reiki energy seems to have an intelligence of its own flowing where it is needed in the client and creating the healing conditions necessary for the individuals needs... The great value of Reiki is that because it is guided by the Higher Intelligence, it knows exactly where to go and how to respond to restrictions in the flow of Ki.* (William Lee Rand, "Reiki Energy:" Reiki.org, http://www.reiki.org/reikinews/whatislg.html, 8/24/2010)

There's the energy balancing of Acupuncture. Reiki does what the needles do in Acupuncture. They stimulate and open the body to the free flow of Qi. The problem though, is that God's method of healing and health is through the blood.

I have read also that it is common for people to get sick and have nightmares after their first Reiki attunement. Sounds like the first night after my wife was muscle tested with the NAET treatment.

It should come as no surprise though for you are dealing with unclean spirits plain and simple.

One story I read of a lady writing into a blog for information and help. She seemed a little disturbed for after introducing herself to the blog, she then went into what happened to her the night after she had been to her first lovely Reiki attunement. She said that it left her shattered, she had a nightmare and a fitful night of sleep. A number of others responded to her with many of them declaring the same types of happenings to them such as nightmares, fear, anger and a beast to live with, and so on. The funny thing was that they all said it was normal and just part of the cleansing process of Reiki. Yet, according to Reiki experts the energy of Reiki always does good. It never is bad.

Satan came to Eve and his first word was, "Yea." He is very positive, isn't he?! Look at the tree Eve. It's good for food. It's good to look at. It's good to be made wise. It's good... it's very good. Oh, dear reader, but it was the tree of the knowledge of good...and evil. That is real balance.

Do you know what a Poppet is? In witchcraft a poppet is a small doll that is used to perform magic on in some ones' place, much like a Voodoo doll. Did you know that some Reiki doctors will hold a small doll, or Teddy bear in their hands and do Reiki on it to treat a person that is many miles away?

The following is a quote from a Reiki master, Christopher Penczak, who is also a practicing witch. Did you know that the Apostle Paul wrote to Christians to warn them that witchcraft is a work of the flesh? He wrote that in Galatians 5:19-21.

> *These tools can also be used to make poppets, or dolls, used to represent someone else. These images can then be used to heal.*
>
> *For those not ready to make their own voodoo dolls for healing sessions, a pillow or even a plush toy can be used as a surrogate. Reiki Masters encourage the use of surrogates when doing distant healing sessions. It gives the healer something on which to focus. This isn't just for Reiki, however. It can be used in most magical forms of healing, visualization, and intent.* (Christopher Penczak, City Magick: Urban Rituals, Spells, and Shamanism, York Beach, ME, Weiser Books, 2001, P. 138) Brief Bio: Christopher Penczak is a practicing witch, Reiki Master, Essence Consultant, and an active spiritual teacher. He is a contributor to many national and local pagan journals and publishes the newsletter, "The Second Road". He lives in New England.

The following ad is from a training school for Reiki. There are two degrees of Attunement programs before this one, but this one shows the training for making a Poppet. Also notice the last class to expand your frequency and bandwidth. It is obvious then, in Reiki you are taking in (like a receiver on a radio) a signal, also known as ki, or an unclean spirit.

I am only showing the third initiation, but there are two levels before the third, and a forth level after it. It is this third that mentions the poppet.

Adkins Alternative Care- Reiki Training

Reiki Training Programs
3rd Degree Initiation (Spiritual)
$400.00
Four week course, approximately 12 hours total
Third Degree Curriculum:
You will receive four attunements
You will explore additional techniques
You will learn Byosen scanning
You will learn beaming
You will create a Reiki poppet
Third degree expands your frequency and Bandwidth
http://www.adkinsalternativecare.com/Training.html

Chapter

6

VIBRATIONAL MEDICINE

Thousands of people sit in the grand stands. The sky is blue; the bright sun shines and warms the people even more on this already warm day. Majestic trumpets sound, the crowd stands to its feet and thousands cheer as the matador is introduced to the people.

Standing tall and proud in glittering clothes and traditional black hat, he lifts his hand and waves heroically and bravely to the people. Armed with only a muleta, which is a red cloth, and some hand spears, he strides out into the dirt arena to face and fight a large, strong, angry, long deadly horned bull.

As the door is opened the caged animal is free to enter the arena, which he does anxiously. All is new to him. Frustrated and angry he is now free to roam the arena not knowing what lies ahead. He is only aware of the sound of thousands of people, and he has a confused sense that something is wrong which makes him defensive and angry. Now in the arena he sees the Matador and the red cloth hanging down. It is shaken as a loud taunt, "Toro, Toro" from the matador is cried.

The bull, in a rage, lowers his head, points his horns, and begins to charge the cloth with a desire to kill the matador. Then as he hits the cloth, there is nothing there. Out the other side and he looks around as if to say, "Where did he go?" Confused and frustrated he looks around to see the matador again. The people are cheering, yelling and clouds of dust are floating around the arena as the bull begins to charge again, only to find nothing as he go through the muleta. But this time a sting is felt on his back, it is the sting of the spear, and it is stuck in the back of the bull.

The bull is still confused, but now senses something is wrong and a fury builds in him to survive, to win, and to live. He sees the matador again, and charges with another sting felt in his back. The crowd cheers as they watch the matador play the bull like a cat with a mouse. Again and again, the bull charges only to find nothing. The blood is flowing swiftly, his strength is growing weak, and finally he collapses only to die to the cheers of the thousands of people who have watched the masterful manipulation by a man with only a cloth and some spears, of an animal that could kill him in an instant if he realized it wasn't the red cloth, but it was the one holding the cloth. It was a deception, and it caused the bull to focus on the wrong thing, which ended in his death.

Somewhere, perhaps America, perhaps Europe as well as other places, is a man or a woman. Their physical weight is heavy. You could say that they are fat. They have tried to lose weight, and are frustrated that they have not been able to make any progress. At times they get depressed, other times discouraged, as they have tried many diets, all to no avail. Then they hear of a new diet. One that has worked for many and it proclaims that you won't be hungry, and you can lose one to three pounds a day. And best of all, when you have reached your desired weight you will be able to keep the weight off because you will not be hungry like you were.

With a slight skepticism they learn more, wanting to be sold that maybe this is the answer they have been looking for after so many years. They read more about it and read the success stories. Little by little the skepticism turns to hope and desire. Yes, it says it is natural, safe, and best of all it works.

What am I talking about? It's the hCG Homeopathic diet. You see the muleta is the hCG, and Homeopathy is the Matador. What is hCG? Well, hCG stands for Human Chorionic Gonadotropin, and it is a hormone that is found in pregnant women's urine. Yes, you read that right, it is found in pregnant women's urine. This definitely would fall under the category of *"profane and old wives fables!"* (1 Tim. 4:7)

Well, according to Homeopathy, hCG, which is produced in great amounts in pregnant women, though it is produced in women and men as well, but the higher concentrations of it in the urine of pregnant women is sought. This hormone is responsible for then increasing your metabolism to the rate of a pregnant women and thus burning off the fat, while you also stay on a 500-calorie diet. That's 500 calories a day.

On and on, as you read about this "amazing" diet, you read of the effects of hCG. But there is just one problem. Like the muleta the charging bull runs through only to find there is nothing there, so too, with Homeopathy when you take the hCG, there is no hCG in the bottle. Zip, Zero, Nada! There is none of it there. All you are taking is milk and sugar.

Welcome to the world of Homeopathy, a system of medicine that is not there. Well, the system is there, but the medicine that claims to have bits of plants, hormones, metals, and other substances is only milk and sugar, for the ingredients that they claim are in there are not in there. They talk like the ingredients are in there, and the ingredients are not in the medicine, but they know that. Confused? *Toro, Toro, Toro!!!* Someone is calling you.

To a Homeopath, or someone who uses Homeopathic medicine, it doesn't matter, for they believe that there is an energetic presence in the medicine, which is far more powerful than the physical presence of the original material.

Like the other medical systems already discussed, as well as the divination methods, when tested under controlled scientific conditions, Homeopathy falls apart. But, as with the other systems, when used in the office, and instructed by Homeopathic doctors and healers, the medicine can work. Again the difference is that familiar spirit. To start with let me explain how Homeopathic medicine is made.

Lets say you have some urine in a jar from a pregnant woman. Kind of a sick thought, isn't it? You might say it is profane! Well, let's say you have some and you wanted to make some hCG diet medicine. First you would have to extract the hCG from the urine. I do not know if the Homeopaths do this, as it is a very expensive procedure with sophisticated equipment. But let's say they do extract the hCG from the urine.

So now you have some pure hCG. On the bottle that I looked at there were these numbers, 12X, 30X, and 60X. The first number means that they took one unit and diluted it with nine neutral units. This would be one X. But then the product must be given its power, so it has to be shook, accentuating the downward stroke about 40 times. Then it has to be pounded against a hard surface another 40 times, such as wood, and something that won't break the bottle but will jolt it real good. Now it can be called 1X.

Then one unit is removed from that bottle and placed into another nine units and now that bottle is shaken and pounded, 40 shaking, preferably downward, and 40 pounding. It is now 2X. Dilution upon dilution, shaking and pounding with each step takes place until you come to 12X. So now, the dilution has one trillionth of one percent in it. In other words there is absolutely no hCG in it at all. The next number on the bottle is 30X, and then 60X.

So this means that there is some solution that has been diluted to 12X, and some more that has been diluted to 30X, and then some more that has been diluted to 60X and they all are mixed together in the bottle and you are to place some drops under your tongue for it to work. What are you placing under your tongue? Physically you are placing water, or whatever the base is, but spiritually, now that is another story. A story that will reveal the true nature of this supposed harmless medical system called Homeopathy.

At the core of this "alternative medical system" lurks an old familiar face. One that we have mentioned already in this book, and it is the face of vitalism. The old belief that foundational to life is the vital force. In every living thing there is a vital force that is at the root of its living, its life and existence. This belief is Satanic in origin for at the root of every living thing is Jesus Christ for the word of God says that He upholds *all things by the word of His power.* (Heb. 1:3) You are upheld by the Lord Jesus Christ, not by some vital force. I know I am repeating myself, but at the root of all of these, "*clouds and wind without rain*" (Prov. 25:14) is this idea of a vital force.

The real force is Jesus Christ, but when they get into this vital force they are into satanic realms of major deception and anti-biblical practices that grieve and quench the Spirit of God according to Galatians 5.

In the making of Homeopathic medicines there is a procedure that they do in order to capture the vital force of a thing. Also know as the Aura, Ether, or Qi, Ki, Prana and any of the other 90 or so names, this "energy" is the source of healing and power in the Homeopathic remedies. At least this is what the founder of Homeopathy, Samuel Hahnemann believed.

> *Hahnemann reasoned that there is a subtle energy force in the body, the vital force, that responds 'to the tiny provocations of the remedies and enable the body to heal itself' (Lockie and Geddes, 1995, p.18). In this respect, homeopathy is compatible to meridian therapies in that both are professed to treat an inherent bio-energy system.* (Fred P. Gallo, Energy Psychology, Boca Raton, CRC Press, 1999, P. 44)

However, homeopathy cannot be understood as a substance based method, such as drug medicine or herbalism where any healing effect is due to chemical reactions. A simple calculation shows that in the higher potencies not a single molecule of the original substance will be present. But these high potencies are often more effective than low potencies. Therefore, homeopathy can only be understood as working with energy remedies.

The explanation is that every natural substance has an etheric field around its molecular structure. The special shaking action or potentizing

> *used in homeopathy separates the etheric fields from their material substance. The latter is then discarded and the former concentrated. These concentrated etheric fields are much more potent in this way than when they were combined with matter. Similar etheric concentrates can be produced with radionics instruments. The healing effect of such concentrates depends on their vibrational frequency. Because of this the name vibrational medicine has been coined for these methods.* (Walter Last, Homeopathy, Health-Science-Spirit, http://www.health-science-spirit.com/Homeopathy.html, 8/25/2010)

So you have this substance, whatever it may be. And this substance has an aura around it, for, according to them, all substances have auras, including rocks as well as live things. This Aura is what they are trying to capture in the Homeopathic remedies, so they take one unit of the substance, like one drop, and they place it in nine, or ninety-nine, or nine hundred ninety-nine, (No I am not kidding) and they then shake it to, as Walter Last says, separate "the etheric fields from their material substance."

> *During the potentization process the substance is "succussed." What happens when the substance is succussed is that it is vigorously shaken and banged on a hard*

> *surface. Hahnemann believed that this "caused the remedy's energy to be released into the water/alcohol mixture."* (Fred P. Gallo, Energy Psychology, Boca Raton, CRC Press, 1999, P. 44)

It has always amazed me that they think this, if there is one, etheric field can so easily be collected. Just shake the Ether, the Aura, the Qi, off of the substance, and then throw the substance out and keep the Ethcr. You now have an energy blue print of the original substance. So, even though there is no substance of the original material in the remedy, there is the energy of that substance and it is far more powerful than the original stuff...at least according to Hahnemann and the leaders of Homeopathy.

There is a problem though, according to Dr. Stephen Barrett:

> *If the FDA required homeopathic remedies to be proven effective in order to remain marketable—the standard it applies to other categories of drugs—**homeopathy would face extinction in the United States**.*
>
> (Stephen Barrett, M.D., Homeopathy: The Ultimate Fake, Quackwatch, http://www.quackwatch.org/01QuackeryRelatedTopics/homeo.html, 8/25/2010).

Again, this energy, which is really spirit, is the same as Acupuncture, Chakras, Reiki, as well as any other variation of energy medicine that is based on the vitalistic view of reality. I say "spirit," yet do rocks have spirits? I imagine some types of people would say so. I know I was reading an article the other day about two New Age, middle aged, women who went on a day hike in Sedona, Arizona, and one of them stopped at a dead tree that was beside the path and prayed to it, asking it for permission to pass by. She said the tree was dead but that its spirit was still present so she prayed to it.

The following is quoted from one of the top five, and at times the top website on Holistic medicine with "*over 4 million hits/month, has clients from over 170 countries in all continents, and is the recipient of several awards. It is undoubtedly one of the most admired websites with a very loyal and passionate following.*" (About Us, International Cyber Business Service, Inc., http://www.icbs.com/about.htm, 8/25/2010)

> *Homeopathic remedies are believed to work in the spiritual plane as opposed to the physical plane as we are used to think and measure. Hahnemann believed that dilution and succussion released a spirit- like power that worked on the spiritual level of the vital force in humans.*
>
> *Homeopathy is an energy medicine, as are acupuncture and therapeutic touch.*
>
> *Homeopaths believe that it is the energy or "vibrational pattern" of the remedy, rather than the chemical content, that stimulates the healing*

by activating what Hahnemann called the Vital force. Vital force is the healing power or energy that exists within us all. It is called by the name Chi by Chinese and Prana by Indian.

(Dr. Jacob Mathew, Chief Editor, How do Homeopathic Remedies work?, Holisticonline, www.holisticonline.com/Homeopathy/homeo_how_it_works.htm, 8/25/2010).

Homeopathy, like the rest of the New Age medicines, is dealing with the supposed bio-energy system, but in a different way for this system is what is know as vibrational medicine. Of course in traditional Chinese Medicine, the Tao is non-vibrational energy, and when it gave birth to Yin and Yang then Yin and Yang are vibrational. Like the old song, "I'm pickin' up... not so good vibrations..." Homeopathy is said to affect the vibrational energy of the body to jolt it from a state of "dis-ease," which is less power, to a state of higher resonance, or greater ease.

Do I need to repeat myself? Well, let me just say that your health and the life of the flesh is in the blood, not in your electron orbitals. Beware of oppositions of science falsely so-called.

It is interesting to note that according to Walter Last, when you shake the substance you are to accentuate the downward stroke. This would mean that you thrust your hand downward faster and harder than when you bring it up. And then you have to bang it downward on a hard surface. It is strange to think of this etheric substance as being subject to gravitational, and centrifugal force. But they say you are to use a downward stroke.

I was then thinking about muscle testing and realized that the majority of the time the indicator muscle is pushed downward. I then read where in the practice of Acupuncture, that when they insert the needle into the body of someone they have to wait for the arrival of Qi. The way they can tell if the spirit Qi arrives is that they will feel the needle pull downward like a fishing pole.

> *Lyrics of Standard Profoundities says; 'It seems a fish bites on fishing pulling the line downward.' This is a vivid description to whether the arrival of qi is obtained or not.* (Cheng Xinnong (Chief editor), Chinese Acupuncture and Moxibustion, Beijing, China, Foriegn Languages Press, 1987, P. 326)

I then remembered a film I saw on the Charismatic movement where the people that were having supernatural manifestations would convulse forward jerking their head downward, and then up, and then down. I then thought of the head bangers listening to Heavy metal, or even hard rock, and the head is jerked downward to the music. Isn't that strange? There is something about that downward jerk.

When a person in a Christian Bible Believing church gets filled with the spirit of God their hands go up, and their face goes up, and they may even jump upward in their joy. You could say that their spirit was lifted.

It should be no surprise that this medicine would align itself with the occult for by very nature vitalism is metaphysical in nature and thus beyond the realm of the scientific. All of the medical practices that are vitalistic in their foundation will be metaphysical and thus lead to, if not outright be, witchcraft. That is its nature and you can not change that no matter how much you pray over your medicine.

Modern Magick:

> *Vibratory Formula: It has long been an occult secret that all matter is made of vibration. Today many scientists depend on this being a fact in their research. If we follow this assumption that all matter is vibratory energy, then magick becomes a type of science which allows a person to affect vibrations. It becomes very valuable for us to develop an understanding of how to control vibratory energy. The techniques for doing this are called Vibratory Formulae.* (Donald Michael Kraig, Modern Magick, St. Paul, Minesota, Llewellyn Publications, 2004, P. 42)

Energy Psychology:

> *Homeopathic theory suggests that humans are somewhat like the electrons of an atom. Electrons within an atom occupy energy shells or spatial domains which are known as orbitals. Each orbital possesses*

> *certain frequency and energetic characteristics depending on the type and molecular weight of the atom. In order to excite or move an electron into the next highest orbital, one needs to deliver to it energy of a specific frequency. Only a quantum of the exact energetic requirements will cause the electron to jump to a higher orbital. This is known as the principle of resonance, in which tuned oscillators will only accept energy in a narrow frequency band. Through the process of resonance, energy of the proper frequency will excite the electron to move to a higher level or energy state in its orbit around the nucleus.* (Fred P. Gallo, Energy Psychology, Boca Raton, CRC Press, 1999, P. 44)

We have now jumped into the world of "vibes." You know, crystals, and meditation, and soaking up the vibrations of a place, as in Sedona. You are right back into witchcraft, and it is a work of the flesh according to Galatians 5:19-20. Even if you are a preacher's wife who treats the church with Homeopathic remedies, you are practicing witchcraft.

I have read in more than one place where Christians who are using Homeopathy say something to this effect, "Well, we pray over the medicine and ask God to take any devils away, so we know it's OK."

Rev. William J. Schnoebelen:

> *Now, all this would make us flee from homeopathy like the plague IF it were a spiritual healing system. However, it does not appear to be spiritual. If it was, it would have been stopped by praying against evil spirits in Jesus' name.* (William J. Schnoebelen, Straight Talk #37 On Homeopathy (revised), Dubuque, IA, With One Accord Ministries, 1999, P. 15)
>
> Bill is an internationally recognized speaker and author of seven books and countless booklets, articles and tracts. He is also a Naturopathic doctor, a Nutritional Herbologist and a Certified Natural Health Professional. Bill is listed in Who's Who in Religion. He was gloriously saved by Yah'shua the Messiah (Jesus Christ) in 1984.
>
> (About Bill Schnoebelen, http://www.withoneaccord.org/About-Bill-Schnoebelen_ep_39-1.html, 8/25/2010)

Well, Bro. Schnoebelen has a problem, for if there is no physical presence in the medicine what else could it be? He states that it could be something far greater than we can understand at this time. Or maybe it could be-but he doesn't know. The problem is that by it's very nature it is wrong and yes, it is spiritual.

> *Homeopathic remedies are believed to work in the spiritual plane as opposed to the physical plane as we are used to think and measure.*

(Dr. Jacob Mathew, Chief Editor, How do Homeopathic Remedies work?, holisticonline, www.holisticonline.com/Homeopathy/homeo_how_it_works.htm, 8/25/2010)

Let me give you an example. Lets say a well meaning, good godly Christian sits down with a New International Version of the Bible. As they get ready to read they bow their head and pray for he Lord to bless as they read the Bible. If the Lord does bless, He will direct them to get a King James 1611. But as far as blessing them through that version, though they may get saved, and a few basic truths, yet by its very nature that version of the word of God is Satanic. If you don't believe me check out Isa. 14:12 with Rev. 22:16 where the New International Version gives Satan the title, "morning star", which is a title given to Jesus Christ. That is blasphemous! This is only one example and if you want more information see any of the books by Gail Riplinger, Sam Gipp, or Peter Ruckman. Because by its nature it is wrong, you can pray over it all day long and it won't change the fact that it is wrong.

When I first got saved I remember one night talking to a young man who said he had gotten saved recently as well. He had been raised a Roman Catholic and was now saved yet trying to reconcile his new found spirituality with the church he grew up in. The problem though, is that Bible Salvation and Catholicism do not mix. A person gets saved in spite of the Roman Catholic Church, not because of the Roman Catholic Church. The reason is because salvation is a free gift, and Roman Catholicism teaches works are necessary for salvation.

As we talked and rejoiced with the news of each other's salvation it grew time for us to leave. As we bowed our heads he prayed and asked God to give them a spiritual Pope. Well, you can pray all you want but you are not going to get a spiritual Pope. If he is truly saved and spiritual, he won't last long. Some sort of accident will come along and he will be gone.

The very nature of the way Homeopathic remedies are made shows that you can pray until you are blue in the face and you will not get rid of the occult presence that permeates the remedies. What will happen is that God will convict you of your sin and deal with you on the need to repent and turn away from this medical witchcraft.

To the skeptic they may look at the method of manufacturing and claim that they are merely placebos created through elaborate methods to satisfy the minds of the partakers, but when you read what they claim it is then you have entered into the spirit realm, and the spirit of Homeopathy is not the right spirit. It is the same spirit of Traditional Chinese Medicine, Hinduism and Reiki.

Hahnemann himself wrote about this supernatural change that takes place when the Homeopathic remedies are made in the Organon, #269 (The "Bible" of Homeopathy):

> *This remarkable transformation of the properties of natural bodies through*

> *the mechanical action of trituration and succussion on their particles (while these particles are diffused in an inert dry or liquid substance) develops the latent* ***dynamic*** *powers previously imperceptible and as it were lying hidden asleep in them. These powers electively affect the vital principle of animal life. This process is called* ***dynamization*** *or* ***potentization*** *(development of medicinal power), and it creates what we call* ***dynamizations*** *or* ***potencies*** *of different degrees.*
>
> (Dr. William.E.Thomas, DYNAMIZATION – POTENTIZATION OF MEDICINES IN HOMEOPATHY., Angelfire, http://www.angelfire.com/mb2/quinine/dynamization.html, 8/25/2010)

Yes, I know, that is about as dry as cracker juice! So let me explain what he just said. He said that there is a "remarkable", in other words magical, change that takes place of the "natural bodies", which just means the stuff like urine, puss, plants, or whatever other profane items they can find, are changed by soaking them in alcohol and water, and then beating on them for a while. Through this process it is claimed there is a power that has been "latent", in other words asleep, and through the process of Dynamization-making it spiritual in nature instead of physical-the sleeping power is awakened. It is this power that will "affect the vital principal of animal life", in other words it will work on or stimulate your, Qi. I guess you could say they are waking Kundalini, or similar to that.

In regards to the dynamization of Kundalini notice the following statement from a woman's personal story of awakening Kundalini:

> *When Kundalini is struck, she awakens, uncoils (i.e. is dynamized), and begins to rise upwards like a fiery serpent, breaking upon each chakra as she ascends, until the Sakti merges with Siva in lay-yoga (laya = absorption), in deep union, samadhi or enstasis.* (Cathy Woods, A PERSONAL STORY OF AWAKENING, cit-sakti.com, http://www.cit-sakti.com/story/kundalini-awakening-story-chapt4.htm, 8/25/2010). (Author sites quote from: Kundalini: the Arousal of Inner Energy by Ajit Mookerjee)

Homeopathy and Yoga have much in common in that they both use a striking force to energize the treatment. While Yoga claims the serpent power of Kundalini, yet Homeopathy claims the Etheric power, or Qi, Ki or Prana, which power is identical to Kundalini.

Hahnemann believed that disease as well as the remedies themselves were spirit like and could not be discovered, so what you have again is called a "curious art" in Acts 19:19, and in terms of modern science this is metaphysical, so there is an element that is beyond provability in this world, for it is out of the physical realm. The blessing for me is that I have the final authority for all such nonsense and it is the King James 1611, the inerrant word of God. Homeopathy is a "curious art" and if you repent you will need to burn all your medicine and books on it.

> *Hahneman, Organon #269, ... triturating a medicinal substance and shaking of its solution (dynamization, potentation) develop the medicinal powers hidden within and manifest them more and more or if one may say so,* ***spiritualizes the material substance itself.***
>
> (Samuel Hahnemann, 6th Edition translated by Boericke, Hahnemann's Organon of Medicine, Homeopathyhome.com., http://www.homeopathyhome.com/reference/organon/organon.html, 8/25/2010)

"Triturating" means immersing the substance so as to extract the contents. Well, look there, the founder of Homeopathy states that the remedies are spiritual in nature. We have just crossed into the occult.

Your medicine should be physical medicine to treat a physical body. This is not the case with homeopathy, but it is very subtle and deceptive. Even more so than the Eastern religious medicines for it is obvious through their origin and beliefs, but Homeopathy claims to be "scientific" and it is not! Homeopathy claims to be natural, and it is not! Homeopathy is supernatural medicine, and therefore is by nature occult. Yes, hello, you are dealing with witchcraft. You know, in Galatians 5 witchcraft is mentioned as a work of the flesh and it lusts against the Spirit of God. You need to repent!

> *To find the cure, that's to say, the herb for the original tincture of the preparation, the researchers often have recourse to occult practices such as the pendulum. Dr. A. Voegeli, a famous homeopathic doctor, has confirmed that a very high percentage of homeopaths work with the pendulum.*
>
> (H. J. Bopp, M.D., Homeopathy Examined, logosresourcepages.org,http://logosresourcepages.org/NewAge/homeopat.htm, 8/25/2010)

Along with this, the newfound "energy" has a mind of its own.

> *The cure alone really knows the patient, better than the doctor, better than the patient himself. It knows just where to locate the originating cause of the disorder and the method of getting to it. Neither the patient nor the doctor has as much wisdom or knowledge.*
>
> (Dr. Baur, Swiss Journal of Homeopathy No. 2/1961, p. 56) H. J. Bopp, M.D., Homeopathy Examined, logosresourcepages.org, http://logosresourcepages.org/NewAge/homeopat.htm, 8/25/2010)

Well, look at that! That is the same claim that the practitioners of Reiki make. The energy/spirit has an intelligence of its own, just like in muscle testing as well. Perhaps it is all the same thing! Perhaps it is all witchcraft disguised in various ways to deceive and beguile the unsuspecting person. Surely, you know that Hinduism is wrong, and Taoism is wrong, but Homeopathy is scientific and natural. It's not religious so I'm safe with this one. Oh no you're not! You are dealing with witchcraft plain and simple. That quote shows that you are dealing with a god, and it is a false god. Just as with Yin and Yang, and all the rest, you are dealing with idolatry and the gods of the land. You are again, committing spiritual fornication against your Saviour. You are back in the spiritual situation of Baalim.

I have already quoted some from William J. Schnoebelen, but I must once again quote from his pamphlet on Homeopathy. The reason is because this man is a Christian and, from what I can tell, believes the King James 1611 is the word of God. I know that is no guarantee your doctrine is pure, but no doubt there are other Bible Believing Christians going to him for advice and getting messed up in witchcraft. It is interesting to note that in the first pamphlet he came out with, about 10 years before this one, on Homeopathy he stated that what's in the Homeopathic medicines is bottled demons. I must say he was closer to the truth with that first one.

In regards to the power of the remedies having their own intelligence he quotes from another work, and keep in mind this is a Bible Believing Christian and he is for Homeopathy, even though about ten years earlier he was against it. We will pick up the quote after he has explained how the remedies have been diluted, and the process of the diluting.

> *Now it should be obvious that you are not drinking simple herbs anymore. In point of fact, there couldn't possibly be any herbs left in these mixtures. Instead, Homeopaths claim that vital power from the tincture is transferred to the remedy through the "potentization"—-through shaking them. The "vital spirit" is said to correct the imbalance of the vital force within the patient. It is almost as if the vital "intelligence" within the plant can talk with the vital "intelligence" within the human cellular structure and bring relief. 10"* (William J. Schnoebelen, Straight Talk #37 On Homeopathy (revised), Dubuque, IA, With One Accord Ministries, 1999, P. 9-10)

I have listed the reference number here for one reason. The reference in the Straight Talk bibliography is merely a comment by Schnoebelen, which reads as follows:

Lest this sound too "spooky,"

No it's not that it's spooky, it's because it is witchcraft; no different than the power of Reiki, and Bro. Schnoebelen is trying to defend his favorable outlook on Homeopathy, which he can not do.

> *...Realize that for generations conventional herbalists have determined that certain herbs, like comfrey and sanicle, seem to be guided by some rudimentary form of internal intelligence once they are ingested. (sic) The herbal preparation* ***goes just where it is needed the most****, in just the right amount to help facilitate healing. This shouldn't surprise us, since the Lord God did make herbs for humanity's benefit. (Gen. 1:30)* (William J. Schnoebelen, Straight Talk #37 On Homeopathy (revised), Dubuque, IA, With One Accord Ministries, 1999, P. 18)

I will get into Herbology in the next chapter, but the first thing to notice is that he is trying to defend this notion that the energy of the remedies of Herbology has its own intelligence. As one author put it, you have now crossed into the realm of a god. And as far as herbs, the herbs in the word of God are for food, not medicine. *And to every beast of the earth, and to every fowl of the air, and to every thing that creepeth upon the earth, wherein there is life, I have given every green herb for meat: and it was so.* (Gen. 1:30) Many of the herbs used in herbology are not even green, and many of the herbs in herbology you would never eat for they would make you sick. Herbs in the Bible are always a reference to food. (Rom. 14,

Ex. 9, 10) The only place even remotely close to herbology is the lump of figs placed on Hezekiah's boil. (2 Kings 20:7)

Bro. Schnoebelen is messed up, and he got messed up when he believed the unbiblical teachings of vitalism. The mystical force of vitalism is satanic in nature. The true force of the universe is "the word of His power." In other words you are held together by Jesus Christ. (Heb 1:3)

Homeopathy is a very dangerous occult practice. It is disguised as scientific and it is not. It is used much like regular medicine in that you take it through your mouth, which is very easy and natural. Of course Adam and Eve got messed up by putting something in their mouth. What's more is that Homeopathy is claimed to be natural, and it is not. It is supernatural or spiritual in nature, and it doesn't matter how much you pray over it, by its very nature it is wrong, for it is a false god.

Can you imagine a couple of Christians pulling out and sitting in front of an Ouija board and praying, "Dear Jesus, if there are any demons in this would you please take them away and guide us so we can find the answer. In Jesus Name, Amen." And then they continue on. If the board works God did not answer their prayer. And if it does not work He did answer their prayer.

If you pray over your Homeopathic medicine you will have one of two things happen; either it won't work, or God will show you the truth and lead you to repent and get rid of it all. If it works and you continue on with the medicine, then you have already rejected light and need to repent. If you are in such a situation you are on your own. In Galatians 5 the answer is to repent, and then the Spirit of God will lead you. *If we confess our sins, He is faithful and just to forgive us our sins, and to cleanse us from all unrighteousness.* (1 Jn 1:9) Being right with Jesus Christ is far more important than your health. Besides, it is not hard for Jesus Christ to heal you, or he may lead you to a real doctor, but either way you must get out of the satanic medicine that you are partaking of.

Aromatherapy and Essential Oils

> *And God breathed into man's nostrils the breath of life, and man became a living soul. (Gen. 2:7)*

Man's spirit is his breath and it is in his nostrils. Your breath is in God's hands.

> Dan. 5:22 *And thou his son, O Belshazzar, hast not humbled thine heart, though thou knewest all this; 23 But hast lifted up thyself against the LORD of heaven; and they have brought the vessels of his house before thee, and thou, and thy lords, thy wives, and thy concubines, have drunk wine in them; and thou hast*

> *praised the gods of silver, and gold, of brass, iron, wood, and stone, which see not, nor hear, nor know: and* ***the God in whose hand thy breath is****, and whose are all thy ways, hast thou not glorified.*
>
> Job 12:10 *In whose hand is the soul of every living thing, and* ***the breath of all mankind.***

When God says you are not going to take another breath then you are not going to take another breath and you are dead.

Some have used:

> Job 3:11 *Why died I not from the womb? why did I not give up the ghost when I came out of the belly?*
>
> Job 10:18 *Wherefore then hast thou brought me forth out of the womb? Oh that I had given up the ghost, and no eye had seen me!*

These two verses have been mentioned to me to prove that man has his spirit before he is born and therefore your spirit is not merely your breath, but that is a faulty way of looking at the text. Both of these texts use the term, *"out of the womb."* The context then of each of these verses is that the baby dies at birth out of the womb, not in the womb. If you don't believe me on this notice Job 3:16 *Or as an hidden untimely birth I had not been; as infants which never saw light.* That is a description of a child that dies in the womb and is what we would term a miscarriage.

So scripture with scripture shows that your spirit has to do with your breath, and your spirit is the energy of your body as stated in James 2:26 *"As the body without the spirit is dead."* Your spirit is your breath as well as your energy, as well as your life. Rev. 11:11 *And after three days and an half the Spirit of life from God entered into them, and they stood upon their feet; and great fear fell upon them which saw them.* Once you loose your breath, you loose your energy and thus your life leaves your body.

As I have mentioned, your medicine should stay on the physical level, or in the physical realm. When you use spirit medicine to treat your physical body you are out of balance. At least you do not find that in the word of God, except when a prophet, such as Elisha, or Jesus Christ himself is healing people. Obviously in both cases it is right. But in this Age of Grace both of those situations are not taking place. Yes, Jesus Christ may heal you just by praying and asking Him to, and if that happens, praise the Lord for answered prayer, He obviously has more work for you to do for Him before He calls you home.

But when you begin to inhale "vibratory frequencies," or in a less technical term, "the life of a plant" or the "energy" of a plant, then you are outside the realm of the word of God, and you are now dealing with your spirit, or a spirit. Thus by nature it is spirit medicine. This is exactly the realm of aromatherapy. You are dealing with aromas and thus you are dealing specifically with your spirit.

In regards to the vibratory frequencies, did you know that your thoughts can change the radio frequency of an essential oil? In Alternative medicine they believe the vibrational frequencies of things need to be balanced and brought into harmony with the universe. Well, they have taken and measured the vibrations of essential oils, whatever they may be, and then they had people think negative thoughts towards the oils and the vibrational frequencies slowed down. The "life force" of the oil grew weak. They then had the people think positive thoughts about the essential oil and the vibrational frequencies increased and the "Life Force" grew strong.

Let me preface a little more about this. True essential oils are alive, in that they have the "life force" in them. Again this life force is the same as Qi, Ki, Kundalini, Innate Intelligence, Prana, Aura, Ether, and the other 90 names for it. It is an unclean spirit, or at least associated with an unclean spirit.

> *The therapeutic value of the oils is dependant on this life force, which is present when extracted properly. These oils, they claim, also contain intelligence.* (Dr. David Stewart Ph.D., The Chemistry of Essential Oils Made Simple: God's Love Manifest in Molecules, Marble Hill, MO, Care Publications, 2005, P. 445, 146)

Hello! Here we go again with Kundalini, or Reiki. Isn't it amazing how all of these various medical arts claim the same thing? The methods may differ, but the "essence" of it all is the same; it is an unclean spirit and a deceptive satanic system at work. It is the gods of the nations that you are warned against in the word of God.

Well, these essential oils that contain this life force when extracted properly, which also has its own intelligence, can get their feelings hurt. According to David Stewart, who claims to be a Christian minister:

> *We respond to the thoughts and prayers of others, whether we are aware of it or not, and so do essential oils. In some of Bruce Tainio's work, discussed in Higley's book, essential oils were measured before and after being bombarded with negative thoughts. Their frequencies went down by 12 MHz. (Do I hear an AAAAHHHH, POOOOR oil! My comment.) When positive thoughts were aimed at the oils, their frequencies went up by 10 MHz. When the oils were prayed over, their resonate frequencies went up by 15 MHz. Oils amplify intent. And intent will move molecules of oil to where they can best serve to heal. That is why prayer and anointing with essential oils work so well when combined together.* (Dr. David Stewart

Ph.D., The Chemistry of Essential Oils Made Simple: God's Love Manifest in Molecules, Marble Hill, MO, Care Publications, 2005, P. 445)

Keep in mind the word "intent," for it is intent that is used by witches to enchant herbs. This will be covered in the next chapter.

> Ex. 30:25 *And thou shalt make it an oil of holy ointment, an ointment compound after the art of the apothecary: it shall be an holy* ***anointing oil****... 31 And thou shalt speak unto the children of Israel, saying, This shall be an holy* ***anointing oil*** *unto me throughout your generations. 32 Upon man's flesh shall it not be poured, neither shall ye make any other like it, after the composition of it: it is holy, and it shall be holy unto you. 33* ***Whosoever compoundeth any like it, or whosoever putteth any of it upon a stranger, shall even be cut off from his people****.*

You had better not be anointing anyone with oil in this age, you may end up dead, and James is written to the twelve tribes of Israel. James 1:1 James, a servant of God and of the Lord Jesus Christ, to the twelve tribes which are scattered abroad, greeting. You had better read your Bible. Besides, essential oils contain an unclean spirit similar to Homeopathy and are associated with witchcraft. Can you imagine someone praying for God to heal him or her all the while they are participating in witchcraft? They are committing spiritual fornication, while at the same time asking their Saviour to help them. That's like a man committing adultery on his wife right in front of her, and then asking her to cook his supper.

> *Essential oils...when energized by our bodily and* ***spiritual forces*** *they vibrate with a spectrum of frequencies that are a unique combination of ourselves and the oils.* (Dr. David Stewart Ph.D., The Chemistry of Essential Oils Made Simple: God's Love Manifest in Molecules, Marble Hill, MO, Care Publications, 2005, P. 184)

So according to Dave Stewart, the oils can be energized by "spiritual forces." Then an unclean spirit certainly can energize them when they are extracted. Wicca and Occult author Scott Cunningham states:

> *Herb magic* (As in witchcraft! My comment) *is a specialized form that utilizes the power of plants. This is the realm of incense, oils, baths, brews and tinctures.* (Scott Cunningham, The Complete Book of Incense, Oils & Brews, St. Paul, Minnesota, Llewllyn Publications, 2004, P. 3)

In the Bible there was a certain man whose son was lunatic. In other words he had a devil, *Matt. 17:15 Lord, have mercy on my son: for he is lunatick, and sore vexed: for ofttimes he falleth into the fire, and oft into the water.* Because of this, and also *Matt. 12:43 When the unclean spirit is gone out of a man, he walketh through dry places, seeking rest, and findeth none,* it looks like devils enjoy warm wet places, and they do not enjoy dry places. My guess is they don't enjoy the cold either.

But in a common extraction process of essential oils they put the plants in a special container and warm them with steam, but the steam cannot get too hot or it will ruin the oils. The plant material is then distilled very slowly for a number of days. The oils come out of a real nice warm wet place. What a great opportunity for devils to "energize" those essential oils. You then "breathe" these oils right up your nose. *And God breathed into man's nostrils the breath of life.* (Gen 2:7) You are dealing with, or should I say defiling your spirit when you breathe in these essential oils, and working in the spirit realm.

They claim the olfactory sensations in the nose resonate to the provocations of the essence of the essential oil, and they attempt to make it sound physical in it's operation, and while there may be truth in the blood brain barrier physiologically, yet it comes in through your nostrils, and aromatherapy is recommended to be inhaled through the nostrils with the mouth shut. Thus you are working in the spiritual realm. Aromatherapy is a spirit medicine just like the other Eastern medicines. It is a bridge to the spiritual realm.

Consider the following advertisement from a website of a very educated oriental instructor and healer:

> *Aiki Healing Chinese* **essential oil** *formulations are available at our holistic online store.*
>
> *Our proprietary formulations are based on the protocols by Jeffrey Yuen, LAc.,* ***Taoist priest*** *of the Jade Purity Tradition.*
>
> *Chinese aromatherapy differs from western aromatherapy in that Chinese aromatherapy blends are prepared with attention to identifying and healing the root patterns associated with illness and other imbalances.* (Notice - Energy balancing again.)
>
> *As a result, Chinese aromatherapy can mitigate constitutional issues at a very deep level, especially when essential oils are applied to specific acupressure points.*
>
> *Constitutional issues include:*
>
> **Genetic tendencies (e.g. A family tendency toward cancer, high cholesterol or diabetes)*
>
> **Patterns that develop in the prenatal state and early years of childhood such as sensory disorders, language challenges and autism.*
>
> **Emotional patterning and personality predispositions.*

***Issues related to one's spiritual journey or soul curricula.** (Kay Hutchinson, Aromatherapy: a Chinese herbal approach, aikihealing.com, http://www.aikihealing.com/aromatherapy.php, 8/25/2010)

Well look at that last one! You are in the spiritual realm aren't you!

While I know it is not an absolute proof, and I would not recommend this, but you can go to the Wicca and witchcraft web sites, and read their books all day long and they will mention essential oils, and aromatherapy. They do not mention Jesus Christ, or the blood of Jesus Christ, or praying to the Lord Jesus Christ, or reading the King James Bible, or attending Bible believing churches, but they do mention Meridians, Chakras, Reiki, Applied Kinesiology, meditation, herbs, Homeopathy and any of the other alternative medicines.

Consider the following trap.

They say emotions and thoughts affect your "vital energy." Negative thoughts can put your "vital energy" out of balance thus opening you up to disease. In Wicca they make a point for you to stay away from negative thoughts for, they claim, that you will get sick if you have them. This is a slick way to keep you away from the word of God for the word of God is negative towards man. You must deal with sin, Hell, judgment, death, Satan, right and wrong. Yes, there are positive things in the word of God, but most of them are only available to those who have been born again. The only positive thing for a lost person is the death, burial and resurrection of Jesus Christ, and even that is negative in nature, except for the resurrection.

As people deal with spirit medicine, they open themselves up to unclean spirits, which bring in negative thoughts and emotions; this in turn brings in fear of sickness. Thus an addiction of sorts is begun in that there will be a need to get thc balance restored through some sort of energy medicine, which in turn brings in more unclean spirits and with them more fear, sadness, and negative thoughts. The person spirals downward in health, or spiritual darkness away from Jesus Christ and the word of God.

Essential oils, as one way, are used to change your consciousness and psyche so as to keep you positive and happy. With the internal darkness that is brought in, you become dependent on your aromas for your emotional condition. This is completely unscriptural and sin. Yes, I said it is a sin and I will tell you why.

Since witchcraft is a work of the flesh, it has an effect of quenching the Spirit of God who, if you are born again, dwells within your body. Your body is the temple of the Holy Ghost if you are saved. If not, your body is the temple of the unholy ghost Eph 2:2, *...the spirit that now worketh in the children of disobedience.* But if you are saved, and you quench the Spirit of God then you may start using these essential oils, among other things, to "lift your spirits." You are attempting to counterfeit the work that is supposed to be done by the Spirit of God who dwells in you.

> Galatians *5:16 This I say then, Walk in the Spirit, and ye shall not fulfill the lust of the flesh. 19 Now the works of the flesh are manifest, which are these; Adultery, fornication, uncleanness, lasciviousness, 20 Idolatry, witchcraft... 22 But the fruit of the Spirit is* ***love, joy, peace,*** *longsuffering, gentleness, goodness, faith, 23 Meekness, temperance: against such there is no law.*

The first three fruits of the Holy Spirit are very positive. Much of New Age and alternative medicine is a quest for the first three fruits of the Holy Spirit. The best thing you can do is examine yourself in light of the word of God and go down the list of the works of the flesh. Confess your sins where you fail and get up and go on. You will find love, joy and peace as well as the other fruits will begin to show forth in your heart and life on their own, for without Him ye can do nothing. You must abide in the Vine. (Jn 15:4)

For me personally, before Terri and I repented of our involvement with Eastern religious medicine, I was usually not in the best of moods. That is not to say that I was never happy, for I was, but now that I have repented there is a great difference. You see, I am not able to walk in the Spirit on my own, and I am not able to produce those fruits of my own will. I am still corrupt, being that I am still in this flesh. But when I repented there has been a great revival in me. I say a revival, and yet, I believe what it really is, is that the Spirit of God is not quenched like He was.

Am I still wicked? No doubt! Do I still sin? Every day! And every day I need to repent, confess my sins, directly to my Saviour, Jesus Christ, and not through some man. I am not talking about sinless perfection. I am saying that if you have been into this witchcraft and repent, you will find that there is a fountain of joy that springs up from the inside, as well as peace, gentleness, and the rest of the fruits of the Holy Spirit. You will not need, nor even desire the effects of aromatherapy. You will probably be convicted if you even try to use it. It is better to surrender and rest in the arms of your loving Saviour, Jesus Christ, than to worry and fear as you attempt to holistically doctor yourself.

The holistic realm is made up of many different methods of attempting to "jolt" yourself electrically, or energetically. Homeopathy and Aromatherapy are two that I have gone into some detail about. There are others as well, such as Bach flower remedies, Sound therapy, color therapy, as well as many others. All of these are based on the same foundation, which believes that if you can affect the energy, and thus the vibrations then you can be healed, or in good health. This is contrary to the word of God, for the life of the flesh is in the blood.

Chapter

7

WITCHCRAFT

Now I have made accusations that these various alternative medical systems of treatment are nothing more than witchcraft; why do I say this? Is it just because witches use these various systems as well? Is that why I claim they are witchcraft? If it were, it would be a very weak argument that would not hold up to any scrutiny whatsoever.

If Christians use these systems of medicine does that make this medicine Christian? Is the determining factor who uses it; or is it something more? Something that is not determined by who uses it, but by what is being used, and how it is used that makes the determination.

The Bible says that, "*whatsoever is not of faith is sin.*" That is quite a statement! The Bible also says that, "*faith cometh by hearing, and hearing by the word of God.*" So that which is outside of the word of God is not of faith. But that has to be qualified as well, for cars are not found in the word of God and there is a group of people who do not drive cars. The difference though is that travel by physical means is still in the physical realm. What's more is that traveling as such is not warned against in the word of God. Telephones, electric lights, airplanes and so on are not found in the word of God either.

There is a whole list of sinful works of the flesh given in Galatians 5, and included in that list is witchcraft. That is what makes it different than merely guilt by association. It is a work of the flesh that is directly opposed to the Holy Spirit of God. Some people who claim to be witches obviously commit this act, and other people who claim to be Christians commit it also. After all, Galatians is written to Christians, not the lost.

I remember one day talking to a Christian man who had been dealing with a Mormon about the need of salvation and the heresy that the Mormon Church taught. He was frustrated "to the max" because of dealing with the Mormon man whose responses to refute the word of God were shallow, yet he would not listen and reason with what the scriptures had to say. As he attempted to refute the scriptural arguments he said, "Jesus Christ had twelve apostles, and the Mormon Church has twelve apostles, therefore we are the right church." This Christian man said to me afterwards, "Yes, and my car is red, and that barn is red therefore my car is a barn!"

Mere association is not a strong enough argument to show, or prove, that alternative medicine is included in the term witchcraft in Galatians 5:19-20. But this chapter, as well as what you have already read, should be sufficient to show that I am not merely using guilt by association. What is being practiced is the use of divination techniques as well as unclean spirits to perform supernatural feats of revealing knowledge and enhancing physical health. The physical aspect is lacking for there is no true scientific proof to the efficacy of these medical practices and systems. All they can do is point to the results and proclaim, "see, it is repeatable, it is repeatable, therefore is must be scientific."

When I sat in my living room in May of 2009 and sensed the peace, love and joy of the Holy Spirit like I had not sensed in a long time, my curiosity was peaked as to what was going on? What was this medicine that had quenched the Spirit of God in our home as well as in our bodies? I sat on the couch that afternoon, dazed and amazed at the change in myself, and at the subtly, deadly treatment that we had just been exposed to. I did not think at the time that it had anything to do with witchcraft. The thought of witchcraft never even entered my mind.

At that time, I did not know what witchcraft was. If I had been asked, 'What is witchcraft?' I suppose I would have said worshipping the Devil. I had not studied witchcraft much at all at that time. I had studied some on the death metal and heavy metal rock and roll bands. I had studied some on sacrifices, for I had grown up due east of San Francisco in the Sierra Nevada mountains, and the Satanists would come up into the mountains to offer their sacrifices, so to me a witch was a Satan worshipper. The Temple of Set, with Michael Aquino, in San Francisco, as well as Anton Levey, and the First Church of Satan in San Francisco was what I associated witchcraft with. To me it was Satanistism, and yes, it is, but that is the black witchcraft. There is the other side that is far subtler, and this is what is killing many Christians in these last days the Laodicean church period.

That small amount of knowledge that I had gleaned over the years was really all I wanted to learn about the subject. I did not want to write this book for I knew I was going to have to study quite a bit about witchcraft and wickedness; and it is something that I do not enjoy, nor have a desire to do. The Bible says, *...I would have you wise unto that which is good, and simple concerning evil.* (Rom. 16:19) As such I had not studied witchcraft at all, at least not this kind.

I would rather study about my Lord and Saviour Jesus Christ, how He left Heaven and died for me so that I could be saved, how He loved me when I was unlovely and ungodly. I enjoy studying about the time when the King of the universe, Jesus Christ is coming back to this earth and take over this world for one thousand years to rule and reign on this earth for that time. I like to study how the Christians will come back with our Lord Jesus Christ on white horses and take over this earth with Him in that day. I like to study of Heaven and my new body that will never sin again, and how there will be no more sorrow, sickness or pain. On and on I could write but to study and write about wickedness and witchcraft is not my desire.

I've had to read wickedness just to find the quotes needed to show the true nature of this New

Age medicine. Along with those dissertations, at times are wicked pictures. So I must fight, quote scriptures, plead the blood of the Lord Jesus Christ and pray my way through. At times I have had to quit, for I was not in a condition to fight as I dealt with the satanic junk that is associated with witchcraft.

In this present time the world is run by the god of this world, which is Satan. *For we wrestle not against flesh and blood, but against principalities, against powers, against the rulers of the darkness of this world, against spiritual wickedness in high places.* (Eph. 6:12) It is a battle, and for those who are already saved, we already have the victory through our Lord and Saviour Jesus Christ. But there is still the command to fight the good fight of faith.

The common Christian who loves the Lord Jesus Christ does not know about the dark things of this world. There is no desire to learn about them either, for it is joy to walk with their Saviour and friend who loved them more than anyone ever has and ever will. There is such a peace and joy to rest in Jesus Christ, but this rest has to be tempered with the command to be vigilant, be sober, because your adversary the devil, as a roaring lion walketh about seeking whom he may devour. Many Christians are resting, sleeping, and relaxing in Jesus when they need to be sober and vigilant. The result is that many Christians in our day are getting devoured by the devil, all the while thinking that everything is fine between them and their Lord.

Do they love their Lord and Saviour Jesus Christ? In this there is no doubt! But they have been deceived and eventually destroyed. Little by little their joy has left, as well as their peace for the flesh has been pampered and primped. Thus the Holy Spirit, the Comforter, has been quenched by the flesh, which has so greatly lusted against that Holy Spirit. Works of the flesh have crept in little by little and the Holy Spirit has been quenched more and more so that they now are in darkness. They have lost their joy and peace and are not getting anything out of their Bible reading and prayer, if they are even doing those things anymore. Often those spiritual exercises have ceased as well.

What's the solution? Repent! If you have been participating in witchcraft, which is specifically what this book is about, then you need to repent. Get on your knees by yourself and confess your sins to Jesus Christ. You are going to have to surrender to be sick, like the apostle Paul did in 1 Cor. 12:8-10 when he stated, *"For this thing I besought the Lord thrice, and He said unto me, my grace is sufficient for thee. Most gladly,* (Did you get that?) *Most gladly therefore will I rather glory in my infirmities that the power of Christ may rest upon me. Therefore I take pleasure in reproaches in necessities for Christ's sake, for when I am weak, then am I strong.* Are you willing to become weak for Jesus Christ?

These prosperity doctrine preachers are led by the devil. This preaching that it is not God's will for you to be sick! One of the greatest Christians in all of the word of God carried a personal physician with him because of his sickness.

Well, let me get back to the issue. As I became aware of the wickedness of this alternative medicine I asked myself, "When is the last time I heard of a Christian getting caught up in witchcraft?" I was saved in 1977 and over those years I had never heard of any Christian getting messed up in witchcraft except for young boys playing role games like Dungeons and Dragons. One teenager I knew, who was also a preachers son, and getting the rest of the young boys in the church interested in the game ended up dead after getting hit by a car in a freak accident.

Just because (I had, and have not) heard of Christians getting caught up in witchcraft, does that mean it does not happen? As I thought to myself I reasoned, *"well of course not, flesh is flesh, and Galatians 5 is just as applicable today as it was in the dark ages, or all of the past 2,000 years."* Then I realized, especially as I studied more, that this alternative medicine is an extremely subtle, camouflaged form of witchcraft. The only way it can be made manifest to the world for what it truly is, is by the word of God. *For whatsoever doth make manifest is light.* It is the word of God that reveals what is truly going on.

In each of the medicines already discussed the outcome is contrary to the word of God. Such as exaltation of self, with your mind and thoughts directed towards self and your body. There is also a friendship with the world and the earth. There is a use of spirits, though disguised as energy. And there is a rebellion towards faith and submitting to the Lord Jesus Christ. But can those medical systems that seem to do so much good really be witchcraft?

Over the next few pages we will go into the practices of Wicca, as well as what the word of God has to say about them. As you will see, many of the practices of Wicca are identical to the practices of alternative medicine, as well as contrary to the direct word of God and what it says about these things. Yes, you are dealing with witchcraft and it is sin.

Notice how identical this is with Taoism, and thus Traditional Chinese Medicine.

> *Whenever one moves out of the transcendent [deity], one comes into a field of opposites.* (This is the same teaching as Tao splitting and giving birth to Yin and Yang, except this is from a book on witchcraft.) *These... come forth as male and female from the two sides. So by splitting into aspects, deity moves into the field of time, which is where humans exist.* (Notice also the use of the word "deity." This is the unknown god of Acts 17. They describe deity, but do not know the deity they worship.) *Campbell continues: 'Everything in the field of time is dual. The past and future. Dead and alive, all this; being and nonbeing, is, isn't.*

That's pretty heady stuff, but the Wiccan interpretation of the same idea is fairly straightforward. The two main aspects of deity that Wiccans work with-the male and the female-are simply called the God and the Goddess. ***The Wiccan God and Goddess represent yang and yin****, positive and negative, light and dark. Since they are two halves of the same whole, they are separate but never truly apart; they are connected by the polarity. Neither exists without the other. The polarity-the relationship-between God and the Goddess is a central, sacred dynamic of Wicca.* (Thea Sabin, Wicca for beginners: fundamentals of philosophy & practice, Mineapolous, MN, Llewellyn Publishers, P. 26)

Thea Sabin is a professional editor and writer whose work has appeared in numerous publications, both pagan and non-pagan, and is a former newspaper astrology columnist. A practicing Wiccan since her teens, the author received formal training in a British Traditional path and currently she and her husband run a coven of the same tradition. Sabin holds a Masters Degree in Education, is an avid organic gardener and lover of Hong Kong gangster movies. She makes her home in the Pacific Northwest. Wicca for Beginners is her first book. (http://www.llewellyn.com/author.php?author_id=1194).

Well look at that! Yin and Yang are the Goddess and God of Wicca! This is the same dualistic teaching and philosophy of Taoism that is straight out of the pits of Hell. Deity in Wicca is equal to Tao in Taoism, at least according to a highly recommended book by a Wiccan high priestess, which is what I just quoted from. When deity is transcended it leaves eternity, or timelessness and splits into the God and Goddess, the Yang and the Yin. Or in another description non-vibrational energy becomes vibrational energy.

When a Christian uses Acupuncture they are using false gods for help. In other words, they are going to the gods of the land.

> *Deut. 6:14 Ye shall not go after other gods, of the gods of the people which are round about you; 15 (For the LORD thy God is a jealous God among you) lest the anger of the LORD thy God be kindled against thee, and destroy thee from off the face of the earth.*
>
> *Num. 25:1 And Israel abode in Shittim, and the people began to commit whoredom with the daughters of Moab. 2 And they called the people unto the sacrifices of their gods: and the people did eat, and bowed down to their gods. 3 And Israel joined himself unto Baal-peor: and the anger of the LORD was kindled against Israel.*
>
> *2Cor. 6:14 Be ye not unequally yoked together with unbelievers: for what fellowship hath righteousness with unrighteousness? and what communion hath light with darkness?*

> *15 And what concord hath Christ with Belial? or what part hath he that believeth with an infidel? 16 And what agreement hath the temple of God with idols? for ye are the temple of the living God; as God hath said, I will dwell in them, and walk in them; and I will be their God, and they shall be my people. 17 Wherefore come out from among them, and be ye separate, saith the Lord, and touch not the unclean thing; and I will receive you, 18 And will be a Father unto you, and ye shall be my sons and daughters, saith the Lord Almighty.*

Witchcraft, as in Wicca, is a polytheistic religion with tax-exempt status in the United States of America. Though witchcraft is satanic, for it is against the word of God, yet Wiccans do not even acknowledge a literal devil. They acknowledge evil, but not a literal devil. Whether they do or don't does not change the fact that there is a real Devil called Satan. It just shows how deceived they really are.

> *While this is true, we would simply like to clarify that Witchcraft and Wicca, while simular in many respects, are not the same. One can be a Witch, without being a Wiccan, just as a person can be a Christian, without being a Baptist. Wicca is a recognized*

> *religion, while Witchcraft itself is not considered a religion. Thus, Wicca might best be described as a modern religion, based on ancient Witchcraft traditions.* (Herne, What is Wicca, The Celtic Connection, http://www.wicca.com/celtic/wicca/wicca.htm, 8/25/2010)

The word "Witch" comes from the Old English "wicce", fem., or "wicca", masc. meaning sorcerer or wizard. It is obvious to see that the word is associated with Wicca. So for all practical purposes we will concern this chapter on the study of Wicca, and the practices thereof. That is not to say that there are not other forms of witchcraft for there are many. Aside from the Traditional Chinese Medicine, Yoga, Reiki, and other medical versions, there are other witchcraft versions as well, such as the black arts, Temple of Set, Satanism, Voodoo, and many others. But this study will mainly deal with Wicca what is known as witchcraft, wicce creaft, or simply, the craft.

As I have stated earlier in the book, there are many variations and yet they are really all the same thing. The external appearance varies, but the internal workings of the system remain the same. As the word of God states, *there is no new thing under the sun.* (Ecc. 1:9) Generally they will be working with energy (spirits), divination, as well as herbs. Some groups are more violent than others, some groups are more superstitious than others, some groups are more intellectual than others and so on, but in the end they are all the same. Witchcraft is a rebellious act against God for the purpose of becoming your own god.

This is how Satan originally fell. He was lifted up with pride, and envied God's position. He wanted to be God and take over god's place and position so he rebelled and said:

> *Isaiah. 14:12 How art thou fallen from heaven, O Lucifer, son of the morning! how art thou cut down to the ground, which didst weaken the nations! 13 For thou hast said in thine heart, I will ascend into heaven, I will exalt my throne above the stars of God: I will sit also upon the mount of the congregation, in the sides of the north: 14 I will ascend above the heights of the clouds; I will be like the most High. 15 Yet thou shalt be brought down to hell, to the sides of the pit.*

Just as King Saul rebelled against what God had told him to do, so too witchcraft is the rebellious pursuit of power with you at the center of the desire. *For rebellion is as the sin of witchcraft.* (1 Sam. 15:23) It is also against everything God is for, and it is for everything God is against. At the root it is rebellion.

As such Witchcraft is an earth-based religion. It is rooted in the earth and friendly towards the earth, but the word of God states that *the whole world lieth in wickedness.*

1John 2:15 Love not the world, neither the things that are in the world. If any man love the world, the love of the Father is not in him. 16 For all that is in the world, the lust of the flesh, and the lust of the eyes, and the pride of life, is not of the Father, but is of the world. 17 And the world passeth away, and the lust thereof: but he that doeth the will of God abideth for ever. James 4:4 Ye adulterers and adulteresses, know ye not that the friendship of the world is enmity with God? whosoever therefore will be a friend of the world is the enemy of God.

That is just a little of what God says about this world. And yet, in Witchcraft there is a desire to be one with the world and universe. The very act of grounding is the attempt at drawing close to this literal dirt ball. In working the root chakra of Yoga, they press the base of the spine against the ground as the start of Kundalini arousing. In Taoism there is an attempt to become one with the earth, as well as the universe. So too in Homeopathy, Essential oils and so on. It is all an attempt at becoming friendly and unified with the world. This is against the word of God and is a major part of witchcraft.

Wicca is a peaceful and harmonious modern day religion based on the

> *reconstruction of pre-Christian traditions and beliefs originating in the Celtic British Isles. It is a balanced and natural way of life, fostering a oneness with the Earth, the divine, and all that exists.*
>
> *Witchcraft in ancient times was known as "The Craft of the Wise". It was the practice of shamans, medicine men and women who worked spiritually with the forces of nature on all levels. They had knowledge of herbs and medicine, they gave council, and they were the Shamanic leaders of their tribes. They possessed the metaphysical understanding that man is not superior to Nature, but simply one part of the whole, one comprised of many levels, both seen and unseen, material and ethereal. They understood that as we take we must return, in order to maintain balance and equilibrium in our individual lives, and in the Universe as a whole. Herbs, Music and More!*
> (Raven Starhawk Cunningham, What is Wicca, wejees.net, http://www.wejees.net/whatiswicca.html, 8/25/2010)

In witchcraft they acknowledge and work with five elements, which are Air, Fire, Water, Earth, and Aether (spirit). Some teachings only acknowledge the four physical elements. In that list the Aether corresponds to the "Qi" of Traditional Chinese

Medicine, or the "Prana" of Ayurveda, or the "Innate Intelligence" of Applied Kinesiology, or "Kundalini" of Yoga, but now we are talking about witchcraft. The "Aether" of Witchcraft is the same power as that of the other medicines, though it has a different name.

> *The Hindus have five elements-Air, Fire, Water, Earth, and Spirit (akasha). Most Wiccans go along with this view. In fact, the pentagram-the supreme symbol of Paganism and Witchcraft-is said to represent the five elements. Each of the points of the pentagram represents one of the elements according to this view, with Spirit on top.*
>
> *I was taught that Wiccans place Spirit on top of the pentagram, but Satanists place Spirit on the bottom of their inverted pentagram. The idea is that Spirit is either above or below matter. Personally, I think a religion focused on the Earth Mother has no business separating Spirit from matter-the idea that either is better than the other necessitates the belief that they're forever separate. If the Earth is a goddess, then how can matter be separate from sacred spirit?* (Deborah Lipp, The Elements of Ritual: Air, Fire, Water & Earth in the Wiccan Circle, St. Paul, Minnesota, Llewellyn Publications, 2003, P. 14)

You know where you do not find the use of this energy/power/spirit? It is not worked with and is rejected in biblical Christianity. A Christian is to work with the Holy Spirit and that is all. Well let me reverse that. The Holy Spirit is to work with, work on, and is to lead you. What's more, it is to be done by faith, for *whatsoever is not of faith is sin.* If a Christian is working with another spirit in any way then that Christian is practicing witchcraft. The only two spirits in the word of God a Christian is to work with is there own, "my spirit" and the Holy Spirit. The only other two spirits there are is the spirit of the Devil, also known as an unclean spirit, and the spirit of an animal. Witchcraft is working with the unclean spirit, regardless of how you work with it. Whether by medicine, chanting, or herbs, (and you are working with an unclean spirit when you use those things), then you are practicing witchcraft.

Another thing that is common in the realm of witchcraft is that it is mainly females that practice it. This is not a hard and fast rule, for yes, there are many men who are witches, but for the most part witchcraft, or Wicca, is a female practice. King Saul, when he wanted to practice witchcraft called for a woman with a familiar spirit.

> *1Sam. 28:7 Then said Saul unto his servants, Seek me a woman that hath a familiar spirit, that I may go to her, and inquire of her. And his servants said to him, Behold, there is*

> *a woman that hath a familiar spirit at Endor.*

Wiccans at times refer to themselves as the wise women.

> *'Wicca' is an Anglo-saxon word that has several meaning, the first being from the root word wicce, which means 'wise.' (Get it...wise women.)* (Ellen Dugan, Elements of Witchcraft: Natural magick for Teens, St. Paul, Mn, Llewellyn Publications, P. 6)

This is a reference back to the garden of Eden when Satan said to Eve that the tree was desired to make one wise, so she partook and instead of becoming wise, she spiritually died, which is what will happen to you if you practice it. What a thing to liken yourself to.

It was the serpent that beguiled Eve: Adam was not deceived but the woman being deceived was in the transgression. Eve was deceived and thought that she was doing good. Many of the women in witchcraft think that they are doing good, when in reality they are sinning against God and serving the god of this world.

This is why it spreads so well camouflaged as medicine. There is a natural desire to nurture that God put in a woman, and it is a good desire. There is no way a man can nurse the sick like a woman. A woman has a natural ability to care for the sick. A man will never be able to meet the emotional needs of his children the way his wife can.

A young boy or girl is running down a path, trips and skins their knee. Pain radiates from the knee and they begin to cry. Dad looks at it and says, "You'll be OK." Mom looks at it and says, "Oh honey, ouch, that hurts doesn't it? Here, lets clean it up and we'll make you feel all better." She then picks him or her up in her arms and nurses them, holds them and helps them feel better. That's a mother. Men were not made for that. A man is not a woman, and a woman is not a man.

I know that may seem obvious, but we live in a time where that knowledge is missing. A man is not a woman, and a woman will have a tendency to feel things without thinking it through, where a man will study a thing coldly separate from emotion. This makes women more open to deception and as in our study, witchcraft. Witchcraft relies greatly upon feeling.

A woman will desire to nurse the wounded soldier. God said her desire would be to her husband and it is. If she married a poor excuse for a husband then she may resent that, and rebel against it, but that desire is still in her. Her desire will be to her husband. She will desire to help and nurse him, especially if he is a good husband. If he aches, hurts, or suffers she will look for a cure to help him.

I heard the story of a pastor's wife who went into a large bookstore looking for a book on some health problem that her husband was having. As she asked the worker if they had any books on what she was looking for, a man held out his card and said, "I can help you with that." The man was a muscle testing, Iridologist, herbologist naturopath. What he really was, was a witch! She took his card, and ended up taking her husband to him and they have been going ever since, as well as recommending people from the church to go. That church has deteriorated ever since they started going to the "eye witch."

That brings me to this question, "What do witches do?" What is witchcraft and what do witches do?

As I said earlier in this chapter, I do not like studying witchcraft, but I did have to in order to write this book, and especially this chapter. While my studies have not been super deep into it, yet there was enough to show what they do and why it is wrong.

For one, witches practice divination, which is something that I have already covered, but will mention it here as well. You see, the medical systems I have already gone over bear great resemblance to the real thing. In other words, what I have already written on is a form of witchcraft. There is more than one or two methods of divination, there are many. As a matter of fact there are well over a hundred forms of divination, yet they are all doing the same thing. They are seeking hidden knowledge through supernatural means.

Sometimes they use tea leaves, or the lines on the palm of your hand, or the flight of birds, or the entrails of dead fish, or the movement of the clouds, or the iris of the eye, or a crystal ball, and many, many other forms.

Here is an example of what I am talking about from a book on magical herbs by a well known and read author of many Wicca books; Scott Cunningham.

> *Definition: Magic is the practice of causing change through the use of powers as yet not defined or accepted by science.*
>
> *I can cause change by accepted means (by calling a friend on the phone I can find out how she's doing); this is not magic. But when I do not have access to a phone, or my friend does not answer, I can make a sachet of thyme, yarrow, and bay, tie it around my neck, still my mind and, using my herb-fortified psychic powers, discover if she is all right. This is its practicality: magic can be used when no other means are available.* (Scott Cuningham, Cunningham's Encyclopedia of Magical Herbs, St. Paul, Minesota, Llewellyn Publications, 2005 P. 3-4)

This is one example of divination where he seeks hidden knowledge through supernatural means. This is divining with herbs, and there are some things to note about it. The first is the fact that he couldn't stand not knowing. It is a form of rebellion coupled with curiosity, hence the "*curious arts*" of Acts 19. This is the same reason

King Saul went to the witch of Endor. As such he used divination, sinned and brought the Lord's wrath down on him. The author I just quoted from wrote many books on Wicca and herbal magic for good health and so on, but he died in his early thirties and went to Hell.

A Christian is to pray and rest in the Lord Jesus Christ. Which brings me to the second point and that is in order to rest in the Lord you are going to have to exercise faith. The desire to know is not the problem, but it is the over ruling of God to the point that you go around God for the answer. As an old preacher said, *"Heaven is the place for understanding, earth is the place for trust."* This story gives a small example of how witchcraft and divination are not of faith.

It's like a little child saying to mom or dad, "I want to know, I want to know, I want to know," and the reply comes back, "You are not old enough to know. You will just have to trust."

There are many things about your body that you just do not know. If you worry, fear and fret, then you may end up going around God to find out the answer. Of course there is no surety that you are going to get the correct answer, but you might. The problem is you do not trust the Lord, and you are using Satan to get your information. Guess whom you are acting like. You are doing what Eve did in the garden, and it is going to kill you, spiritually first, and then perhaps physically.

If you are reading this and have never been born again, you cannot do what I am writing about. You need to get saved by admitting that you are guilty before God. *For all have sinned and come short of the glory of God. Rom. 3:23* You have sinned against Him, and so have I. As such you are going to Hell when you die. *Rev. 21:6 And he said unto me, It is done. I am Alpha and Omega, the beginning and the end. I will give unto him that is athirst of the fountain of the water of life freely. He that overcometh shall inherit all things; and I will be his God, and he shall be my son. But the fearful, and unbelieving, and the abominable, and murderers, and whoremongers, and sorcerers, and idolaters, and all liars, shall have their part in the lake which burneth with fire and brimstone: which is the second death.*

Jesus Christ paid for all of your sins when He died and shed his blood for you on the Cross of Calvary. *Col. 1:14 In whom we have redemption through his blood, even the forgiveness of sins.* He was buried, and three days later he arose from the grave. *Matt. 28:5 And the angel answered and said unto the women, Fear not ye: for I know that ye seek Jesus, which was crucified. 6 He is not here: for he is risen, as he said. Come, see the place where the Lord lay.* Admit you are lost, believe that Jesus Christ is your only hope, pray and ask Him to forgive you of your sins, come into your heart, and save you from Hell. *John 1:12 But as many as received him, to them gave he power to become the sons of God, even to them that believe on his name.*

If you are saved and have been using divination, such as muscle testing, Iridology, pendulum herbal work, or alternative medicine hair analysis, as well as many other forms of divination, you need to repent. All of these New Age methods of diagnosis are divination because they are not using anything scientific, or operating in the physical realm. These are spiritual practices used in the occult.

This is witchcraft. It does not operate in the physical realm. It is metaphysical in nature. Metaphysical is a relatively new word for it and is more of a politically correct term. The old word was occult. (Paul Tuite'an, Estelle Daniels, Essential Wicca, Berkeley, California, The Crossing Press, 2001, P. 383) You are dealing and working in the occult.

Energy

Another aspect of occult, or witchcraft, is the working with energy. All the way through this book these various systems have a preoccupation with energy. Witchcraft has a preoccupation with energy. In one of his books on witchcraft, William Keith, who is a scientist and a witch states:

> *How does subtle energy fit in with magic? The raising and transmission of energy is,* ***of course****, a major aspect of magical workings. I know from experience that I feel something when I raise energy in-circle...* (William H. Keith, The science of the craft: modern realities in the ancient art of witchcraft, New York, New York, Kensington Publishing Corp., 2005, P. 238)

At the heart of witchcraft and the occult is the raising and working with energy. Notice the ***"of course."*** It is taken for granted that this is one of, if not the main aspect of "the craft", also known as witchcraft. This energy, which is really spirit just as the medical systems use, is equated with power, and that is at the root of this whole thing. Power is the ability to control ones own life, or so they think. But there is no power greater than the Most High God, the Lord Jesus Christ.

When these witches work with power, yes, there is something that truly does take place, but if you consider the power the Lord of the universe has in order to just speak the universe into existence, then the power that these witches are dealing with is mere child's play and pacifiers for the kiddies in order to keep them amused for a while. After that, they will die and go to Hell. Their fleeting moment of power will soon be forgotten in the pit of weeping and wailing and gnashing of teeth.

The Old English definition of "Craft" in the concise Oxford dictionary means, "Strength or Power."

The pursuit of power itself is against the word of God when Jesus Christ said, *"He that humbleth himself shall be exalted."* (Luke 14:22) You are to submit and surrender to the Lord Jesus Christ. This is the opposite of witchcraft. Witchcraft is the pursuit of self-exaltation, independence and thus rebellion against God.

When a person possesses self-discipline and a strong will, then the

> *Wiccan/Witchcraft phrase 'As my will/word, so mote it be!' takes on powerful meaning.* (Raven Grimassi, The Encyclopedia of Wicca and Witchcraft, St. Paul, Minnesota, Llewellyn Publications, 2003, P. 137)

This is the opposite of Jesus Christ when He prayed, *Luke 22:42 Saying, Father, if thou be willing, remove this cup from me: nevertheless not my will, but thine, be done. 1Sam. 15:23 For rebellion is as the sin of witchcraft, and stubbornness is as iniquity and idolatry.*

Along with this rebellious attitude is the fact that what they are dealing with is spirits, and spiritual power. When they are in circle, or divining through crystals, levitating, or any of the other acts that they do, they are doing all of this through unclean spirits, which they view as energy. To a certain extent it is energy. Energy that is limited to the realm they are in. But as this is central to witchcraft so too it is central to every medical system that I have just written about, as well as all of the New Age systems.

Energy, or "Qi," is central to Traditional Chinese Medicine. Energy is central to Yoga and the chakras, as well as Reiki. Energy is central to Homeopathy and essential oils. At the heart of witchcraft, and at the heart of New Age medicine is occult energy. Though called by various names it is all the same thing, has its own intelligence, and adapts to people in different continents so as to deceive them, thus to keep them in darkness for one purpose only, and that is to damn their souls and take them to Hell, or defile them, if they are saved, so they will not be used by God.

Energy is not central to a Christian. Jesus Christ is central to a Christian. He is our energy, power, and Spirit, for the Bible says, *"Now the Lord is that Spirit, and where the Spirit of the Lord is, there is liberty."* (2Cor. 3:17) If a Christian is to seek power then they are to be filled with the Holy Spirit, for the Bible again says, *"...be filled with the Spirit."* (Eph. 5:18) All this witchcraft is counterfeit and fake. The problem is that there are Christians, and some of them are Bible reading Christians who love their Lord Jesus Christ, that are getting messed up in witchcraft. Though it is disguised as medicine, it differs not at all from true witchcraft. If there is any difference it would be in the terminology, but the practice is the same.

If you were to remove the alternative medicines' methods of diagnosis, which you should, because they are divination, then remove energy from the alternative medicine treatments, alternative medicine would dry up and be blown away with the wind.

So too, if you were to remove divination and energy work from Witchcraft it would also be blown away with the wind. That is because they are one and the same. There is no difference. Christians are doing to same things, the same ways, for the same reasons as the witches; it is witchcraft. I know I have said it before, but did you know that witchcraft is a work of the flesh as found in Galatians 5:20?

Herbs

The last activity that I am going to cover in regards to witchcraft is the medical side of witchcraft. Yes, a major aspect of Wicca is the medical aspect. Down through the ages there have been "natural healers" around, and people have gone to them for help. For centuries they have been preached against and Christians have been warned that they were practicing witchcraft. Churches for centuries have preached against it, but now at the end of this night of the church age, the sun is about to rise, and in these twilight minutes just before the rising of the sun, Christians are slipping into witchcraft. Though medical in practice, nevertheless it is still witchcraft. *Now the Spirit speaketh expressly, that in the latter times some shall depart from the faith, giving heed to seducing spirits, and doctrines of devils.* (1Tim. 4:1)

Medicine is one of Wicca's main activities, and what a better way to propagate Satanism than by doing "good."

> 2 Cor. 11:*14 And no marvel; for Satan himself is transformed into an angel of light. 15 Therefore it is no great thing if his ministers also be transformed as the ministers of righteousness; whose end shall be according to their works.*

In the medical books of witchcraft over and over you read natural healing, spiritual healing, cleansing, and natural health. Feel good about yourself. On and on you can read in the Wicca books about the medical methods practiced to enjoy a healthy life.

As energy is central to witchcraft, lets say on the spiritual side of it, so too central to witchcraft on the physical side is herbs. Herbs are central to witchcraft. But they are not the herbs of the Bible, for the herbs of the Bible are different.

You see the herbs of the Bible are always food. They are never medicine. There is one time a lump of figs is used on Hezekiah's boil. If you want to say that is an example of herbal healing in the word of God help yourself, but it is not even close to the oriental herbs and the herbology of our day.

> Gen. 1:29 *And God said, Behold, I have given you every herb bearing seed, which is upon the face of all the earth, and every tree, in the which is the fruit of a tree yielding seed; to you it shall be for meat.*

The herbs of the Bible are for food. Here in Genesis you have the original purpose for herbs and God said that it is for meat, or food.

> Gen 1:30b *I have given every green herb for meat.*

Exodus 9:25...*the hail* ***smote every herb*** *of the field...*

Ex. 9:31 *And the* ***flax and the barley*** *was smitten: for the barley was in the ear, and the flax was bolled.*

Ex. 9:32 *But the* ***wheat and the rie*** *were not smitten: for they were not grown up.*

Ex. 10:12 *And the LORD said unto Moses, Stretch out thine hand over the land of Egypt for the locusts, that they may come up upon the land of Egypt, and eat every* ***herb of the land, even all that the hail hath left****.*

Rom. 14:2 *For one believeth that he may eat all things: another, who is weak,* ***eateth herbs****.*

So here you have four herbs mentioned, and at one point in their growth they are all green, by the way. Flax, Barley, wheat and rie are all herbs according to the word of God, and they are for food, not medicine. The herbs in Romans 14 are obviously food. *For one believeth that he may eat all things: another, who is weak, eateth herbs.* (Rom. 14:2)

Though brief, this is enough to show that in the word of God herbs are for food. Now I am not saying that it is a sin to use herbs for medicine, and a little further on I will give some guidelines to use if you are going to use herbs for medicine. But what you need to see right now is that the

Alternative Medicines' use of herbs does not fit with the use in the word of God. Though there are herbs mentioned in the word of God, and I am talking about the typical herbs of today, yet it should be noted specifically how they are used, for you will not find them used the same way that they are used in Wicca and any of the other medical systems of witchcraft.

Herbs in Wicca, as well as other forms of witchcraft play a major role in the practice of witchcraft. Without herbs, witchcraft would be severely cut back in its practices, for many of the practices, especially the medical practices, are performed with herbs. Herbs take up a major place in the Wicca books, as well as on the Wicca web sites. I have found it interesting what has been written about herbs in some of these books, and web sites as well.

> *Enchanting Herbs*
>
> *Prior to actually using herbs in magic, they can be enchanted. Enchantment (in a magical context) aligns the vibrations of the plants involved with your magical need. Thus it is a process, which increases the effectiveness of the herbs.*
>
> *Enchantment may be performed on a single herb or a mixture, but should not be done until moments before the herb is to be used. When several herbs are needed for a spell they may be enchanted together*

> *as a mixture or singly as each herb is introduced into the mixture.* (Scott Cunningham, Cunningham's Encyclopedia of Magical Herbs, St. Paul, Minnesota, Llewellyn Publications, 2005, P. 11)

There are those, and maybe dear reader, you are one, that scoffs at such a thing, but the author of the book I just quoted is well read and has sold hundreds of thousands of books. These people are very serious about what they do, and they do get results from it all.

When I think of enchanting herbs I can't help but think of the Disney movie "Enchanted." It kind of puts it into a whole new light doesn't it!

Cunningham's Encyclopedia of Magical Herbs:

> *To practice herb magic you must know the powers of the plants. This book contains that information. To fulfill a need, just manipulate the herbs to give their powers direction. It is that simple.*
>
> *Herb magic is easy because the powers (i.e., vibrations) lie in the herbs themselves. No outside forces need be called into play, for the power is resident within the organic matter.* (Scott Cuningham, Cunningham's Encyclopedia of Magical Herbs, St. Paul, Minnesota, Llewellyn Publications, 2005, P. 5)

Well look at that! Here is a very well known Wicca author stating that the power of herbs is their vibrations. No, this is not from a book on

Homeopathy, or essential oils, or Acupuncture, or the chakras, this is an encyclopedia of witchcraft.

Here is another quote from: The Complete Book of Incense, Oils & Brews, by Scott Cunningham:

> *Magic-the use of natural energies to bring about needed change-arose when those early humans discovered invisible forces around them.*

Did you notice they were "natural?" I wonder if they are organically grown too?

> *They felt energies within their own bodies that could be moved according to will and need.*
>
> *The power of magic springs from the Earth itself, as well as from stars and celestial bodies. It resides within winds, rocks and trees; in flames and water and our bodies. Rousing and directing such forces sums up the practice of magic.*
>
> *Herb magic is a specialized form that utilizes the power of plants. This is the realm of incense, oils, baths, brews and tinctures. An act of herb magic may be as simple as rubbing a scented oil onto a colored candle, setting it in a holder, lighting it and visualizing your magical need.* (Scott Cunningham, The Complete Book of Incense, Oils & Brews, St. Paul, Minnesota, Llewellyn Publications, 2004, P. 3).

Magic then, also known as Wicca and witchcraft, which is a work of the flesh that lusts against the Holy Spirit of God, is energy work, and that energy is vibrational in nature. Herb magic includes the use of oils and tinctures. There's your essential oils and the mother tincture of Homeopathy. There's the stimulating energy of the herbs in the meridians of acupuncture, except this is a book on witchcraft written by a Wiccan.

> *"In herb magic-or any form of magic-we must raise and release this energy."*

In Yoga it's called arousing Kundalini, in Traditional Chinese Medicine it's called the arrival of Qi and so on. It's all witchcraft!

> *In magic we work with the universal energies that are channelled through our bodies, through herbs and colors. Because they are universal energies, they are universal in origin, scope and influence.* (Scott Cunningham, The Complete Book of Incense, Oils & Brews, St. Paul, Minnesota, Llewellyn Publications, 2004, P. 6,9).

There's your color therapy, same as with the chakras. Channeled same as meridians.

> *Definitions of words:*
> *Herbalism: The practice of cultivating, gathering and using*

plants for medicinal, cosmetic, ritual, and culinary purposes.

Herb Magic: The practice of directing energies found within plants to create needed change. A branch of magic. Practitioners utilize personal power as well as other forms of energy, such as colors, candles, stones, sounds, gestures and movements. (Scott Cunningham, The Complete Book of Incense, Oils & Brews, St. Paul, Minnesota, Llewellyn Publications, 2004, P. 239)

Stones: There are your hot rocks on the back to balance the chakras.

Gestures: There are the signs drawn upon palms before a Reiki session.

Movements: There are the Yoga Asanas.

Personal Power: The energy which sustains our bodies, and which is available for use in magic. (Scott Cunningham, The Complete Book of Incense, Oils & Brews, St. Paul, Minnesota, Llewellyn Publications, 2004, P. 240)

Well, there is the satanic vitalism doctrine. The energy, which sustains our bodies, is claimed to be Qi, Ki, Prana, Innate Intelligence, Yin and Yang, and many more terms. But this energy is what is used, or claimed to be used in witchcraft, though here it is called magic. It's the same thing.

Any medicine that operates from the vitalistic view is using energy, and the energy that they claim to be using is the exact same energy that is used in witchcraft. Therefore when you use New Age medicine you are practicing witchcraft plain and simple. That is why it is listed as a work of the flesh in Galatians 5. If you have been using energy medicine then you need to repent. It is far more important to be right with the Lord Jesus Christ than to seek physical healing from Satan. *Job 2:4 And Satan answered the LORD, and said, Skin for skin, yea, all that a man hath will he give for his life. 5 But put forth thine hand now, and touch his bone and his flesh, and he will curse thee to thy face.*

Besides, you know that your Saviour is able to heal you right now if He so chooses. *Eph. 3:20 Now unto him that is able to do exceeding abundantly above all that we ask or think, according to the power that worketh in us, 21 Unto him be glory in the church by Christ Jesus throughout all ages, world without end. Amen.*

He can either heal you directly, guide you to the right doctor, or he may want you to stay sick. You may ask why He would want that? It may be so He can use you more.

> *2Cor. 12:7 And lest I should be exalted above measure through the abundance of the revelations, there was given to me a thorn in the flesh, the messenger of Satan to buffet me, lest I should be exalted above measure. 8 For this thing I besought the Lord thrice, that it might depart from me. 9 And he said unto me, My grace is*

sufficient for thee: for my strength is made perfect in weakness. Most gladly therefore will I rather glory in my infirmities, that the power of Christ may rest upon me. 10 Therefore I take pleasure in infirmities, in reproaches, in necessities, in persecutions, in distresses for Christ's sake: for when I am weak, then am I strong.

Chapter

8

CONCLUSION

It was a small store front church just outside the small town in a newly built strip mall. One of the main roads ran right in front of it, so the location was good as well. The young pastor, I'll call John, worked very diligently having to spread his time and energy between his wife and three children, his job, and pastoring the small church. It was, and is, not an easy thing to do.

There was a family there as well who was very dedicated to the service of the Lord. The husband, whom I'll call Jim, was a graduate of a Bible Institute and had come up there in search of God's will for his life. As such he was attempting to serve the Lord in the ministry of helping this new small church to grow and get established.

The work progressed slowly, but this was to be expected, for "it is the last days and people generally do not want the truth." At least that was the mindset. Little by little the church grew, though between work, family and church, Pastor John was pulled in every direction. As it grew then there would be a set back so that the growth tapered off, and so too did the finances.

Jim and Pastor John were close in their friendship and Pastor John was so glad to have Jim's assistance in the work. Jim, his wife and children, were a good solid family and it was refreshing to have them in the church. It was kind of strange though as Jim and his family was often sick. They used health foods and would also use the various alternative medicines and practices, yet they were sicker than Pastor John and his family, and he did none of that medicine.

My first trip to the church went well as I preached, and Terri and I tried, by the grace of God, to be a help and to be a blessing to the people and ministry there. I could see the struggle with work, finances and all. I understood that struggle too, for I had tried four times to pastor; three times I tried starting a church from scratch. I well knew the demand placed on a pastor who has to work, prepare sermons, and still be a father and a husband. I could see all the struggles in Pastor John as he labored out of love for his Saviour, the Lord Jesus Christ.

The next year Terri and I returned for another meeting and it went well, but there was a certain sadness in the church, but especially with pastor John and his family. Bro. Jim had decided to leave and help another church that was many, many miles away. They were going to be leaving the work, and as a matter of fact, the last night of the meeting was going to be their last night in the services. Pastor John did not want them to leave, but Jim believed it was the right thing to do, so that final night we said good-bye, and Pastor John's main helper and assistant said good-bye as well.

It was a valley and a hard time for Pastor John. One that pushed him to his limits as to whether he could continue on with the little store front church. Questions and emotions ran through his mind. His wife as well, was low in spirit for she was very close to Jim's wife as well. Now she would be alone with no one whom she could talk to that would understand the hardships of the ministry. For Pastor John and his family, it was a very hard time.

The next Sunday came, and Pastor John with his family arrived for services. As they opened the storefront church that Sunday, some visitors came. After the service they said they liked it and would be back. Not only that but the offering was better than usual. Though low in spirits, this was a bit of encouragement. It was as if the Lord was saying to Pastor John, "I'm still here. I know what you are going through. I have not left you."

The next Sunday, the new visitors showed up as well as some other people. The offerings were up, and there was a good spirit in the church. Pastor John sensed a new freedom in the service, as well as joy. The people were talking to each other and laughing. It was very encouraging to Pastor John and his family. Soon the discouragement that weighed them down faded away and changed to an attitude of encouragement and hope.

Attendance was growing; the offerings were growing as well. Pastor John could sense in a very real way that the Lord Jesus Christ was very much helping him in this small store front ministry. The small meeting room was soon filled with people from front to back. They were filling up.

I had a very short meeting with them again as I was in the area, and I could tell things were going much better. It was such a change from the last meeting that seemed so gloomy as we departed. After the service we went out to eat. During the discussion, Pastor John asked about the book I was working on, and I told him that I was writing on New Age medicine. At the time I did not know what else to call it. Curiously he and his wife asked for more information about it, so I told them the story of how Terri had been muscle tested and picked up an unclean spirit after the session.

We talked for some time about it all, and then Pastor John mentioned Bro. Jim and how they had been into all of that sort of medicine. He said, "You know, they were sick all of the time." I went on to explain how it is witchcraft and is not of the Lord. Then Pastor got a little quiet; he knew what I was about to ask. I then asked him, "How has your church been since they left?"

Pastor John looked down, but all of a sudden his wife looked at Terri and I with her eyes wide in amazement. Pastor John then said, "I knew you were going to ask that. The very next Sunday they left we had people visit and join the church. Bro. Jim is a good friend, but ever since they left, the ministry has done very well. It has done so well that when he calls I downplay how it's going because a don't want to make him feel bad."

I looked at him and his wife and said, "That's what I'm writing about. It is deadly and killing churches and Christians all over this nation."

Pastor John's wife was speechless. Now, before their eyes, light shone in, and they could see why it had been so hard, why God had been hindered, and why God was now blessing and helping their church. Though they are the closest of friends, yet his helper, Bro. Jim, had been hindering the church because of the medicine that he was using. It really is witchcraft. Witchcraft is a work of the flesh and will quench the Spirit of God; at least that is what the word of God says.

It is no different than having someone in your church that is living in adultery, fornication, idolatry or any of the other sins mentioned in Galatians 5. God will not bless you if you are using this witchcraft that is camouflaged as medicine. It grieves the Spirit of God and steals His help and blessing in your church and life. You must repent and turn from your sin.

It is not a matter of casting out devils. It is a matter of repentance. You need to repent. In order to repent you are going to have to surrender your all to the Lord Jesus Christ, and that includes your health. You KNOW He is able to heal you if He chooses to! You know that. You must now surrender to that.

If you have been using a treatment and you don't know if it is right or wrong, then pray! Ask God to show you if it is right or wrong, and then act on the light He gives you. I've had people ask me if certain treatments are right or wrong and I'll be honest and say, I don't know on certain things. But there is a God in Heaven and he knows. That is for sure! And there is a Bible that is the holy word of God, and it has the answer, that is for sure! If you have been deep into this medicine, then repent and ask the Lord to lead you out.

Study the treatment you have been using and critique it with the word of God. Does it match the word of God? Is it spiritual medicine in its nature, or is it physical in its nature? Study and pray! Jesus Christ has the answer, but you must surrender to His will and His word.

What is the origin of the treatment? Where did it come from? What does the Bible say about it? You may not get an answer right away, although if it is wrong Jesus Christ will give you an answer right away. You will have enough light to know what is right.

This book will give you enough light to know a good amount of what is right and wrong.

Any medicine that uses muscle testing, and divination in any way is wrong. Any medicine that uses supernatural energy in any way is wrong. If you remove muscle testing, divination and energy medicine from your medicine you will eliminate the majority of all alternative medicine practices. If you use herbs according to the Chinese recommendations then you are wrong. The origin is Satanic, and the practice is outside the scriptures.

Remember: The life of the flesh is in the blood, not the energy!

LIST OF SOURCES

Editorial Staff, Ice Age Acupuncture?, Acupuncturetoday.com, http://www.acupuncturetoday.com/mpacms/at/article.php?id=27608,8/23/20

http://www.adkinsalternativecare.com/Training.html

Victoria Anisman-Reiner, "Manual Muscle Testing", naturalmedicine.suite101.com, http://naturalmedicine.suite101.com/article.cfm/manual-muscle-testing-a23265, 8/26/2010

Stephen Barrett, M.D., Homeopathy: The Ultimate Fake, Quackwatch, http://www.quackwatch.org/01QuackeryRelatedTopics/homeo.html, 8/25/2010

Dr. Baur, Swiss Journal of Homeopathy No. 2/1961, p. 56) H. J. Bopp, M.D., Homeopathy Examined, logosresourcepages.org, http://logosresourcepages.org/NewAge/homeopat.htm, 8/25/2010

Beckner M. "Vitalism", The Encyclopedia of Philosophy, P. Edwards, Editor. 1967, The Macmillan Co: New York. p. 253-256. Quoted from the Journal of the Canadian Chiropractic Association, 1998, Volume 42(1)

Berggren, L. (1985) "Iridology: A critical review". Acta Ophthalmologica 63(1): 1-8. University of Cambridge, http://www.cl.cam.ac.uk/~jgd1000/iridology.html, 8/26/2010

H. J. Bopp, M.D., "Homeopathy Examined", Logos Resource Pages, http://logosresourcepages.org/NewAge/homeopat.htm, 8/26/2010

Raven Starhawk Cunningham, What is Wicca, wejees.net, http://www.wejees.net/whatiswicca.html, 8/25/2010

Scott Cuningham, Cunningham's Encyclopedia of Magical Herbs, St. Paul, Minesota, Llewellyn Publications, 2005

Scott Cunningham, The Complete Book of Incense, Oils & Brews, St. Paul, Minnesota, Llewllyn Publications, 2004

Guy Danowski, http://www.betterhealththruresearch.com/Biokinesiology.htm

Gita & Mukesh Desai, from DVD-Yoga Unveiled, Gita Desai, 2004, B.K.S. Iyengar "Guruji"

Donahue J., DD Palmer and Innate Intelligence: Development, Division and Derision, Assoc Hist Chir, 1986, Quoted from the Journal of the Canadian Chiropractic Association, 1998; Vol. 42(1)

Erin Dragonsong, "Applied Kinesiology: Your Body As A Divination Tool", Wicca-Spirituality.com, http://www.wicca-spirituality.com/applied-kinesiology.html, 8/26/2010

Ellen Dugan, Elements of Witchcraft: Natural magick for Teens, St. Paul, Mn, Llewellyn Publications

Donna Eden, Energy Medicine, New York, New York, Penguin Group, 2008

Estes, Charles Sumner (1895). "Christian missions in China" (Thesis (PH. D.) - Johns Hopkins University,1895).Baltimore. OCLC10128918(http://www.worldcat.org/oclc/10128918), http://en.wikipedia.org/wiki/Medical_missions_in_China, 5/15/2010

Foxes Book of Martyrs, Chapter VIII, John Fox, Accordance Bible Program - Public Domain

Robert Frost, Applied Kinesiology, Berkeley, California, North Atlantic Books, 2002

Fred P. Gallo, Energy Psychology, Boca Raton, CRC Press, 1999

Vitalism, P Gove, Editor, Webster's Third New World Dictionary, Springfield, Merriam-Webster Inc., 1993

Helen Graham & Gregory Vlamis, Bach Flower Remedies for Animals, Tallahassee, Florida, Findhorn Press, 1st Indian Edition, 2002

Raven Grimassi, The Encyclopedia of Wicca and Witchcraft, St. Paul, Minnesota, Llewellyn Publications, 2003

Guiley R., Universal life force, Encyclopedia of Mystical and Paranormal Experience, San Francisco, Harper, 1991, P. 626-630, Quoted from the Journal of the Canadian Chiropractic Association 1998; vol. 42(1)

Samuel Hahnemann, 6th Edition translated by Boericke, Hahnemann's Organon of Medicine, Homeopathyhome.com., http://www.homeopathyhome.com/reference/organon/organon.html, 8/25/2010

Haldeman S., Modern Developmants in the Principles and Practice of Chiropractic, ed. Haldeman S., 1979, New York: Appleton-Century-Crofts. 390, Quoted from the Journal of the Canadian Chiropractic Association, 1998; Vol. 42(1)

Herne, What is Wicca, The Celtic Connection, http://www.wicca.com/celtic/wicca/wicca.htm, 8/25/2010

Doug Hoff, "medical dowsing", http://homeoinfo.com/08_non-classical_topics/dowsing/medical_

dowsing.php,, 8/26/2010). (Bio: http://homeoinfo.com/me.php

Kay Hutchinson, Aromatherapy: a Chinese herbal approach, aikihealing.com, http://www.aikihealing.com/aromatherapy.php, 8/25/2010

About Us, International Cyber Business Service, Inc., http://www.icbs.com/about.htm, 8/25/2010

Adam J. Jackson, Iridology: A Practical Guide To Iris Analysis, London, Vermillion Press, 1992

Bernard Jensen & Donald V. Bodeen, Visions Of Health: Understanding Iridology, New York, Avery Publishers, 1988

Bernard Jensen, Iridology Simplified, Escondito, California, Iridologists International, 1980

Bernard Jensen, Iridologists International, Volume 2, Number 7

Bernard Jensen, Iridologists International, Volume 4, Number 1

Denny Ray Johnson, What The Eye Reveals, Boulder, Rayid Publications, 1995, Inside Cover

Keating J, The Evolution of Palmer's Metaphors and Hypothesis, Philosophical Constructs for the Chiropractic Profession. 1992; 2:9-19, Quoted from the Journal of the Canadian Chiropractic Association, 1998; Vol. 42(1)

William H. Keith, The science of the craft: modern realities in the ancient art of witchcraft, New York, New York, Kensington Publishing Corp., 2005

Kurt E. Koch, Occult ABC, Grand Rapids, Michigan, Kregel Publications, 1986

Donald Michael Kraig, Modern Magick, St. Paul, Minesota, Llewellyn Publications, 2004

Walter Last, Homeopathy, Health-Science-Spirit, http://www.health-science-spirit.com/Homeopathy.html, 8/25/2010

Chris Lawson, KUNDALINI ENERGY: Yoga's Power, Influence, and Occult Phenomena in the Church, Spiritual Research Network, http://www.spiritual-research-network.com/yoga.html, 8/24/2010

Deborah Lipp, The Elements of Ritual: Air, Fire, Water & Earth in the Wiccan Circle, St. Paul, Minnesota, Llewellyn Publications, 2003

Henry C. Lu, Chinese Natural Cures, New York, New York, Tess Press, an imprint of Black Dog & Leventhal Publishers, 1994

The Yellow Emperor's Classic of Internal Medicine, translated by Dr. Henry Lu, Vancouver,

BC, Published by International College of Traditional Chinese Medicine of Vancouver, BC, 2004

Mao-liang Chiu, Chinese Acupuncture and Moxibustion, Edinburgh, Elsevier Science Limited, Robert Stevenson House, 1993

Dr. Jacob Mathew, Chief Editor, How do Homeopathic Remedies work?, Holisticonline, www.holisticonline.com/Homeopathy/homeo_how_it_works.htm, 8/25/2010

Rammurti S. Mishra, The Textbook of Yoga Psychology, New York: Julian, 1963, As quoted by Kurt E. Koch, Occult ABC, Grand Rapids, MI, Kregel Publications

Demon Experiences in Many Lands, Chicago, Moody Press, 1960

Devi S. Nambudripad, M.D., D.C., L.Ac., Ph.D. (Acu.), Say Good-Bye To Illness, Buena Park, California, Delta Publishing Company, 2002

Christopher Penczak, Ascension Magick: Ritual, Myth & Healing for the New Aeon, Woodbury, Minnesota, Llewellyn Publications, 2007

Christopher Penczak, City Magick: Urban Rituals, Spells, and Shamanism, York Beach, ME, Weiser Books, 2001

William Lee Rand, "Reiki Energy:" Reiki.org, http://www.reiki.org/reikinews/whatislg.html, 8/24/2010

Elizabeth Reninger, The Meridian System: Channels of Awareness, About.com, http://taoism.about.com/od/themeridiansystem/a/meridian.htm, 8/23/2010

Elizabeth Reninger, "What Is Qi (Chi)?", About.com, http://taoism.about.com/od/qi/a/Qi.htm, 1/21/2010

Thea Sabin, Wicca for beginners: fundamentals of philosophy & practice, Mineapolous, MN, Llewellyn Publishers

Thea Sabin, bio, http://www.llewellyn.com/author.php?author_id=1194

About Bill Schnoebelen, http://www.withoneaccord.org/About-Bill-Schnoebelen_ep_39-1.html, 8/25/2010

William J. Schnoebelen, Straight Talk #37 On Homeopathy (revised), Dubuque, IA, With One Accord Ministries, 1999

Dr. David Stewart Ph.D., The Chemistry of Essential Oils Made Simple: God's Love Manifest in Molecules, Marble Hill, MO, Care Publications, 2005, P. 445

John Thie, D.C. & Matthew Thie, Touch For Health, Camarillo, California, DeVorss& Co., 2007, Quote from trustee for Touch for Health

Dr. William.E.Thomas, DYNAMIZATION – POTENTIZATION OF MEDICINES IN HOMEOPATHY., Angelfire, http://www.angelfire.com/mb2/quinine/dynamization.html, 8/25/2010

Paul Tuite'an, Estelle Daniels, Essential Wicca, Berkeley, California, The Crossing Press, 2001

Merriam-Webster online dictionary, Merriam-Webster.com, http://www.merriam-webster.com/dictionary/divination, 8/26/2010

Cathy Woods, A PERSONAL STORY OF AWAKENING, cit-sakti.com, http://www.cit-sakti.com/story/kundalini-awakening-story-chapt4.htm, 8/25/2010 - Author sites quote from: Kundalini: the Arousal of Inner Energy by Ajit Mookerjee

Cheng Xinnong (Chief editor), Chinese Acupuncture and Moxibustion, Beijing, China, Foriegn Languages Press, 1987

Denise Zimmermann, Katherine Gleason, Miria Liguana, The Complete Idiot's guide to Wicca and Witchcraft, New York, New York, The Penguin Group, 2006

Other Books Available From This Author

HERE COMES THE BRIDE

a critique of the Baptist Bride Heresy

Is a local, Baptist church the bride of Christ? Did John the Baptist start the first Baptist church with Jesus as one of his members? Is a saved Methodist, Lutheran, or Catholic in the bride of Christ? What is the Baptist Bride Heresy?

You may wonder at the absurdity of these questions, and yet the Baptist Bride Heresy is a predominant belief amongst many Baptist churches. From years of experience and much study, Ken McDonald writes to refute this heresy. With actual quotes from such men as Dr. Jack Hyles, Pastor James R. Love, Dr. Thomas Cassidy and others, you will begin to see the seriousness and proliferation of this belief. The author then takes you on, and shows you from the word of God (King James Bible) the faults and deceptions of the Baptist Bride Heresy.

Here Comes the Bride

a critique of the Baptist Bride Heresy

Ken McDonald Th.M

ISBN: 978-0-9798844-1-2, Paperback

Other Books Available From This Author

PURSUIT

one man's quest to find God's perfect will for his life

As one reads this book, the first thing that comes to mind is the fitting title...Pursuit. As Christians, who of us have not wanted to know the perfect will of God for our lives? Brother Ken openly bears his heart as he describes his "hot pursuit" of God's perfect will for his life. Have you struggled...have you searched...have you been discouraged in "pursuit"? This book will encourage you and help you to see that you are never alone in that struggle. "A good read and hard to put down. –Assoc. Pastor H. Getto, CT

A very candid story- one that is hard to put down until you see the victory won! Very insightful for women as it helps us to better understand the thoughts and struggles of a man in pursuit of God's perfect will for his life. –Danilee Varner, pastor's wife, NY

Available at: www.kenmcdonaldfamily.com
www.amazon.com

ISBN: 978-0-9798844-0-5, Paperback

Made in the USA
Charleston, SC
09 November 2013